# TEXAS ENTERTAINERS

BARTEE HAILE

# TEXAS ENTERTAINERS

## Lone Stars in Profile

THE History PRESS

Published by The History Press
Charleston, SC
www.historypress.com



*Front cover, top left*: RGD5F4447, Houston Public Library, HMRC; *top middle*: RGD5F3637, Houston Public Library, HMRC; *top right*: 1949 SMU *Rotunda* yearbook, Houston Public Library, HMRC; *bottom left*: RDG5F7003, Houston Public Library, HMRC; *bottom middle*: RGD5F1009, Houston Public Library, HMRC; *bottom right*: RGD5F1205, Houston Public Library, HMRC.

*Back cover, left*: RGD5F3285, Houston Public Library, HMRC; *right*: RGD57610.b, Houston Public Library, HMRC.

First published 2019

Manufactured in the United States

ISBN 9781467141512

Library of Congress Control Number: 2018963684

*For those Texans who down through years put their hearts, souls and egos on the line to keep the rest of us entertained.*

# CONTENTS

# ACKNOWLEDGEMENTS

The quality and abundance of photographs that provide the reader with a priceless glimpse of the past make the publications of The History Press truly unique. As with my previous books, I struck gold at the Houston Metropolitan Research Center, thanks to the incredible Joel Draut and recently retired jack-of-all-trades Timothy J. Ronk, who lent an expert hand as my consultant. In addition, I am again indebted to Terre Heydari and Anne Peterson with the DeGoyler Library at Southern Methodist University in Dallas for their assistance.

Ben Gibson must have drawn the short straw because he once more served as my editor at The History Press. I can only hope that it was a more pleasant and less painful experience the second time around for the patient and knowledgeable Texan in exile. I definitely look forward to our third collaboration in the near future.

And I cannot say enough about the tremendous contribution of my wife, Gerri Haile. As proofreader on my first book, she has grown into an indispensable editor and gifted researcher whose ideas and suggestions I value most of all.

# INTRODUCTION

Writing a weekly newspaper column on Texas history for thirty-five years teaches you a thing or two about the Lone Star State's past and the people that came before us. One of those things is how many entertainers, famous and forgotten, were native-born or naturalized Texans. Early in my career, I at first noticed and then was genuinely surprised by the sheer number of actors, authors, singers, dancers, musicians and other performers from the Lone Star State.

You would be forgiven for presuming that many, if not most, of the individuals profiled in this collection were born and raised in a big or a mid-size city. Fact is, the majority came from small towns and even tinier communities that barely qualified for a post office; such obscure and remote locations as Tioga, Dinero, Peaster, Indian Creek, Murvaul and Kosse, to name just a few.

This makes perfect sense in light of the fact that everyone in this book was born in the late nineteenth or early twentieth century, when Texas was an overwhelmingly rural state. It was not until the census of 1950 that half of the inhabitants lived in a town with a population of five thousand or more.

Their rustic upbringing gave them a natural down-home appeal that audiences found endearing. Moviegoers could spot a phony from the top balcony of the theater, especially an actor from back East who tried to pass himself off as a Texan. That was why casting directors wanted men who spoke with an authentic drawl and looked like they belonged on horseback for the countless cowboy roles in the hundreds of Westerns.

The same qualities proved to be an asset in country-and-western music. Tex Ritter, Buck Owens, Bob Wills, Waylon Jennings and scores of other singers who did not quite reach icon status made the most of their distinctive "twang."

Texans who never sang a note on screen still managed to make a good living in Westerns. "Big Boy" Williams played a variety of parts in the movies but always seemed most at home as a cowboy. The same was true of Chill Wills, who like "Big Boy" was a born comedian.

Texans, particularly actresses like Corinne Griffith and Madge Bellamy, got in on the ground floor of the motion picture industry during the "silent" era. Joan Crawford went those two giant stars of the 1920s one better by making a smooth transition to "talkies," which extended her career by four more decades.

It is nothing less than remarkable that three of the greatest female dancers in the "golden age" of the Hollywood musical were immensely talented Texans. Their films may be seventy or eighty years old, but Cyd Charisse, of Amarillo; Ann Miller, of Nacogdoches; and Ginger Rogers, of Fort Worth, still light up the screen with their brilliance.

While Texas may not be known as a literary breeding ground, you would not know it from the authors found between these covers. George Sessions Perry, David Westheimer, Alan Drury, Fred Gipson, Robert E. Howard, J. Frank Dobie and Katherine Ann Porter were master storytellers whose works have stood the test of time.

*Texas Entertainers: Lone Stars in Profile* is not a parade of happy endings. Too many of these lives were cut tragically short, several at an early age, by plane crash (Buddy Holly, Jim Reeves and Audie Murphy), car wreck (Johnny Horton), fire (Linda Darnell), suicide (Don "Red" Barry, Robert E. Howard and George Sessions Perry), botched surgery (Dan Blocker) and that age-old scourge, cancer (Carolyn Jones, Roger Miller and Zachary Scott). To this roll must be added a trio of deaths under circumstances so mystifying that foul play has to be suspected: Bobby Fuller, Larry Blyden and Ted Healy.

But this book is less about how these Texans died and more about how they lived and what they achieved. I found each and every one fascinating in his or her own way, and I believe you will too.

—Bartee Haile
August 2018

1

# GENE AUSTIN

## *The Original Crooner*

The popular singer and prolific songwriter, whose recordings sold eighty-six million copies in the 1920s and 1930s, was born Lemeul Eugene Lucas in 1900 in the North Texas town of Gainesville. He did most of his growing up near Shreveport, where his mother moved with her second husband after the death of Gene's father.

Back in those days, restless boys really did run away and join the circus, and the fifteen-year-old was one of them. Finding life under the big top not all it was cracked up to be, Gene went back home but left for good a few months later.

The teen talked his way into uniform by tricking a recruiter into believing he was older than he looked. He kept up the masquerade long enough to take part in General Pershing's pointless pursuit of Pancho Villa before getting kicked out of the Army for being underage.

But Gene dreamed of fighting the Germans in the trenches of France and reenlisted in April 1917, when his birth certificate passed muster. As a bugler, he saw the horrors of the World War I only from a distance and returned to civilian life no worse for the experience.

Gene spent the next four years at a Baltimore college studying dentistry and the law, while devoting his nights and weekends to the piano and the blues. In 1923, he finally faced the fact that music was his true passion and quit school to try his luck on the vaudeville circuit.

To avoid confusion with an established entertainer named Lucas, the aspiring amateur borrowed his stepdad's last name. In spite of a lifelong

Gene Austin's 1950s comeback could not have come at a better time for the over-the-hill singer, who made and spent millions in his heyday. *RGD5F6037, Houston Public Library, HMRC.*

inability to read sheet music, Gene Austin cowrote a hit song with his vaudeville partner before the act broke up.

The talented Texan did not have to wait very long for his big break. In January 1925, Aileen Stanley agreed to record "When My Sugar Walks down the Street" for Victor Talking Machine Company on the condition that one of the three composers join her. Gene's soft voice and understated style convinced the New York cabaret singer they would make beautiful music together.

Stanley proved to have a keen ear. Their duet was magic on vinyl, and Victor could not wait to get Gene under contract and back in the recording studio.

By the end of 1926, the dropout had four best-selling singles—"Yes Sir! That's My Baby," "Five-Foot Two, Eyes of Blue," "Yearning (Just For You)" and "Bye, Bye, Blackbird"—and more money than he ever knew existed. Gene had received a check for $96,000 at a time when the average annual income in America was $1,500.

Music business skeptics, smugly certain the overnight sensation was just another flash in the pan with a short shelf life, soon had to eat their words. Gene's star rose even higher the next year with three more classics: "Tonight You Belong to Me," "Forgive Me" and the incomparable "My Blue Heaven," which sold more records (an estimated five million) than any song in history until Bing Crosby released "White Christmas" in December 1941.

Crosby was one of many famous "crooners" who credited Gene Austin with creating the uniquely intimate style. Credit also belonged to the inventor of the electronic microphone, which revolutionized radio and sound recording after its introduction in 1925.

Big bucks predictably resulted in a lavish, high-on-the-hog lifestyle for Gene and the first of his five wives, Kathryn. A mansion, expensive cars, the latest fashions and partying until dawn in New York's most exclusive nightspots—no one lived larger in the Roaring Twenties than the Lone Star crooner.

Gene came close to not seeing the 1930s. Noticing how much Kathryn enjoyed sailing on a stockbroker's yacht, he bought an even bigger luxury craft and paid the $75,000 asking price in cash.

On the maiden voyage of *My Blue Heaven*—what else?—down the Atlantic coast, the captain suddenly changed course for open water to dodge a dangerous storm. Gene waited for the weather to clear by drinking himself into a stupor, while Kathryn wept hysterically.

When the ship's radio came back on, the first words heard on board *My Blue Heaven* were: "Those were three more songs introduced and made famous by Gene Austin. Once again, we repeat, the Coast Guard has abandoned the search for the famous crooner's boat and all the hands must be presumed to be drowned."

Reports of Gene's death were, as Mark Twain once wrote, greatly exaggerated, but the drastic decline of his career during the Depression was real and painful. Though not compelled to stand in line for food, times were tough on his bank account as well as his ego.

In 1938, Gene turned to a just-off-the-boat Dutch immigrant to get his career back on track. Tom Parker (the honorary title of "colonel" was ten years in the future) neglected to mention that he knew next to nothing about the music business and that Gene was his first client. Although he did not come through for Gene, the invaluable experience prepared Parker for his unbelievably successful partnership with Elvis Presley.

A 1957 television special about his ups and downs gave the aging performer a second chance. Gene Austin took full advantage of the swan-song opportunity by making personal appearances wherever his fans, new and old, would pay to see and hear him and by writing the last of his hundred songs with cancer knocking on the door.

Gene Austin, the original crooner, lost his battle with the dreaded disease on January 24, 1972. Six years later, his 1928 recording of "My Blue Heaven" was inducted into the Grammy Hall of Fame.

2

# GENE AUTRY

## *Singing Cowboy with a Midas Touch*

In tiny Tioga in far North Texas (the population in 2004 was 833), just a hop, skip and a jump from the Red River, Orvon Gene Autry was born on September 29, 1907.

Autry's first paying gig as a guitar-plucking adolescent was with a traveling medicine show. He spent a summer on the road singing tear-jerking ballads, while Dr. Fields peddled his patent cure, "The Pain Annihilator."

But a career in show business did not hold much appeal for a down-to-earth youth like Autry. After graduating high school and moving to Achille, Oklahoma, he went to work for the railroad. He felt lucky to land a steady job and was not about to give up a weekly paycheck for the starvation wages of a struggling entertainer.

A few words of encouragement from none other than Will Rogers changed Autry's mind. The famed humorist happened to drop by the telegraph office in Chelsea, Oklahoma, on a summer evening in 1926 and heard the relief operator practicing his chords. Rogers urged the nineteen-year-old to take his natural talent back East and try to break into radio.

Autry thought about it for a year before using his railroad pass to buy a cut-rate ticket to New York City. Choosing to imitate Al Jolson, he flunked his first audition but heeded a smart piece of advice to stick to his own country-and-western style.

Back in the Sooner State, Autry won a spot on a Tulsa radio program as the "Oklahoma Yodeling Cowboy." The modest success restored his confidence, and six months later, he was ready to scale the heights in Manhattan.

This time Autry made the grade, and in October 1929, the month that the stock market crashed, he cut his first single. In the recording studio that same day were two other aspiring artists, Rudy Valee and Kate Smith, and the three became lifelong friends.

Autry sang his way onto the Chicago-based *National Barn Dance*, forerunner of Nashville's *Grand Ole Opry*. Then in 1931, he struck gold with "That Silver-Haired Daddy of Mine."

During his prolific musical career, Autry recorded over three hundred songs and had a hand in writing at least a hundred more without ever learning to read a note. Other releases that reached the magic million mark included "Back in the Saddle Again," "South of the Border," "You Are My Sunshine" and "Peter Cottontail." None, however, matched the astounding success of a song he had to be hounded into recording.

At the insistence of his wife, Ina May, Autry reluctantly released a Christmas tune in 1949. Two and a half million copies were sold the first year, and by 1977, sales surpassed ten million. To Autry's amazement, "Rudolph the Red-Nosed Reindeer" became a holiday classic.

The established radio and recording star made his film debut in 1934. The white gloves destined to be his trademark were originally worn by the nervous novice to keep his fidgety hands occupied.

The next year, six small movie companies merged to form Republic Pictures. As the studio's box-office workhorse, Autry ground out Saturday matinee Westerns at the rate of one every six weeks. He was the number one sagebrush hero of the silver screen for more than a decade.

A chewing gum manufacturer offered the movie star a radio show in 1940. *Melody Ranch* was an instant hit and stayed on the air for sixteen years.

After the United States entered World War II, Republic moguls assured Autry that strings could be pulled to keep him out of uniform. But he indignantly refused to go along with the unpatriotic plan and sacrificed an annual income of half a million dollars to enlist in the Army Air Corps.

While Autry flew cargo planes, the studio bosses made good on their threat to find a replacement while he insisted upon doing his duty. An unknown actor named Leonard Slye was transformed into Roy Rogers, "King of the Cowboys." Returning from the war, Autry held no grudge against the newcomer and, in fact, prevented Republic from dumping him.

So-called adult Westerns, full of sex and violence, took Hollywood by storm in the early 1950s. Autry's wholesome films seemed dull by comparison and out of step with the times, and in 1953, he appeared in his ninety-third and last motion picture.

Gene Autry with one of three horses named Champion he rode in all his movies and television shows. He bought the original from cowboy actor Tom Mix. *RGD5F4447, Houston Public Library, HMRC.*

Instead of fading into obscurity, Autry burst into Americans' living rooms. He formed his own production company and turned out ninety-one episodes of the *Gene Autry Show* for television.

Retirement for Gene Autry meant devoting his full-time attention and his head for business to far-flung ventures that encompassed hotels, radio and television broadcasting and a major-league baseball team. Although his original interest in the Los Angeles Angels lay in the right to broadcast the team's games, the commissioner convinced him that full ownership was the way to go.

Autry was popular with players and fans alike. Upon his death, the players voted to retire uniform number twenty-six as a token of respect for the owner they regarded as the twenty-sixth Angel.

At his passing in 1998 at age ninety-one, he was worth more than $300 million. Or, as Pat Buttram, his former celluloid sidekick, once joked, "Autry used to ride off into the sunset. Now he owns it."

Today, versatile Gene Autry is the only person honored with all five stars for recording, radio, motion pictures, television and live performance on the Hollywood Walk of Fame.

3

# TEX AVERY

## *Sad Life of Bugs Bunny Cartoonist*

Since his mother claimed to be descended from the "Law West of the Pecos," she christened her blessed event Frederick Bean Avery. He was born at Taylor in 1908 but grew up in Big D, graduating from North Dallas High School.

With his athletic good looks and love of the outdoors, people were always surprised to learn that Fred Avery had his heart set on a career as a cartoonist. The ink was still wet on his diploma when he signed up for a summer course at a Chicago art institute. But after a month of still-life sketching, he packed his bags and caught the next train for Texas.

In the winter of 1928, Avery took a road trip to Southern California with his best friends from high school. When it came time to leave, he told his buddies to go home without him because he had decided to stay in the Sunshine State.

Avery survived for several months by loading produce trucks and falling asleep to the sound of the surf. Recalling his adventure as a stranger in California many years later, he smiled, "You would be surprised how warm and soft a beach is after working all night."

Failing to find a buyer for his comic strip, the Texan went to work as an assistant animator with the Walter Lantz Studio. To him, the ground-floor opportunity was strictly a necessary evil, a way to keep body and soul together until the day he made it big in the funny papers.

But that day never came, and Tex—a nickname coined by unimaginative coworkers—eventually resolved to give animation his best shot. His prospects were decidedly dim due to the freely admitted fact that he was "never too great an artist. Most of those fellows at Lantz's could draw rings around me."

The loss of an eye in a freak office accident put Avery at an even greater disadvantage and permanently changed his disposition. The life of the party with self-confidence to spare was gone only to be replaced by a brooding introvert with a deep inferiority complex.

Convinced he was finished as an artist, Avery jumped at the chance to master every phase of production. He was a dream come true for his lazy boss, who gave the eager beaver everything but his paycheck, including complete charge of two cartoons in his fifth and final year with Lantz.

As soon as his debut flicks were in the can, Avery jumped ship for an all-or-nothing, one-film tryout with Warner Bros. The classic *Gold Diggers of '49* so impressed producer Leon Schlesinger that he hired the twenty-seven-year-old as his third animation director.

For the next seven years, Avery and his madcap crew worked out of a small frame building dubbed "Termite Terrace." Only in retrospect did three-time Academy Award winner Chuck Jones recognize the unique talent of his former boss. "I was as ignorant of his genius as I suppose Michelangelo's apprentices were oblivious to the fact that they too were working with a genius."

Conceding the child market to Disney, Avery appealed to older moviegoers with a frantic gag-filled pace and adult humor that sometimes bordered on the risqué. His wisecracking characters broke the stodgy mold with sarcastic ad-libs and handheld signs that poked fun at the story as well as the audience.

Avery created Daffy Duck, supposedly a native of Dallas's White Rock Lake, and transformed a couple of extras—Bugs Bunny and Porky Pig—into big-time stars. Until the rabbit underwent a personality transplant in *A Wild Hare* (1940), he was "just Daffy Duck in a rabbit suit." Student slang at North Dallas High School inspired Bugs Bunny's trademark greeting "What's up, Doc?"

Angered by a two-month suspension for insubordination, Avery quit Warner Bros. in a huff in 1941 for the greener pastures of Metro-Goldwyn-Mayer (MGM). He more than paid his own way with an average annual output of five cartoons over the next thirteen years.

Although many of his features—*Northwest Hounded Police*, *Red Hot Riding Hood*, *Slap Happy Lion*, *King Size Canary* and *Swing Shift Cinderella*, to name only a few—are considered masterpieces, Avery took a back seat to William Hanna and Joe Barbera, whose *Tom and Jerry* series won seven Oscars. To compete with his rivals, the insecure workaholic rarely went home and even put off trips to the bathroom, a self-destructive habit that on one occasion necessitated the insertion of a catheter to drain his bladder.

When MGM let him go in 1954, Avery was already burned out. While Hanna and Barbera were taking television by storm with their own production company, he spun his wheels for twenty years cranking out commercials. His most memorable contributions to advertising were the "Frito Bandito" and the bugs screaming "Raid!"

Avery's private life was in worse shape than his career. His marriage did not survive the drug overdose death of a son, leaving him to live alone in a shabby apartment.

Tex Avery drew his last breath on August 26, 1980, in the same California hospital where Walt Disney died fourteen years earlier. At his funeral, Avery was eulogized as "a leader who never established a studio, never tried to do anything but make good films." And, most of all, he made millions laugh even though his world was not all that funny.

4

# DON "RED" BARRY

## Troubled Trails of B-Western Cowboy

The future rider of the B-Western range was born Donald Barry de Acosta in Houston in January 1912. Despite his small stature—five feet four and a half inches—he was good enough at football, presumably as a running back, to win a college scholarship.

In one version of how the miniature Texan got his big Hollywood break, John Wayne and Mickey Rooney happened to see him play in an exhibition game between a team of college all-stars and the University of California at Los Angeles (UCLA). The diminutive Rooney, who at five two had to look up to Barry, arranged a speaking part for him in *Boys Town*, but he could not remember his lines, and the director kicked the flustered first-timer off the set.

Barry told a completely different story about his early days in the movie capital that included no mention of Rooney or the blown opportunity. In his account, he wound up in Tinsel Town in the depths of the Great Depression with only one thing on his mind: where his next meal was coming from.

"Food's pretty wonderful any time," Barry reflected, "but you don't know how really wonderful it is until you've skipped meals for as long as I did. I had never acted but never having done something hasn't ever seemed a reason to me for not trying it anyway."

Barry figured all he had to do was to sneak inside a motion picture studio, but that proved to be harder than he imagined. Twice he climbed the high walls of the selected studio, and both times security guards tossed him out on his ear.

Don "Red" Barry (center) sharing a laugh with actor Dennis O'Keefe and an unidentified woman. *RGD5F6622, Houston Public Library, HMRC.*

But the third attempt turned out to be the charm. "There I was inside the studio and not a cop in sight. I walked around as free as air. There were some chorus girls outside a sound stage (so) I stepped up and started rehearsing them. They thought I belonged there, and so did the director when he came over."

Barry's masquerade lasted a brief three days, but he was rewarded for his brashness with a place on the payroll. However, his combative personality, which caused him problems throughout his career, soon cost him that job.

Never one to give up, Barry tried his luck with a road company of *Tobacco Road*. "I fast-talked my way in. When they asked if I'd had any experience (acting) before, I said 'Yes' and changed the subject."

In a matter of months, Barry graduated from stage to screen with the customary bit parts that constituted the meat and potatoes for newcomers. By 1939, he had attracted the attention of Republic Pictures, giant of the low-budget Western, which put him through the usual bad-guy tryout in four pictures that year.

Republic signed Barry to a long-term contract before casting him as Red Ryder in a series of twelve Saturday-afternoon cliffhangers. The temperamental Texan predictably pitched a fit, pointing out the comic strip character was tall and skinny while he was not. The studio boss made it clear that he either did what he was told or he was finished at Republic.

Although Barry hated to admit it, *The Adventures of Red Ryder* was the best thing that ever happened to him. For the rest of his life, he would be known as Don "Red" Barry, not because of the color of his hair but because of the memorable Ryder role.

Long after the Red Ryder serial was in the can, Barry kept grinding out sagebrush soap operas for Republic at the rate of two per month. But he wanted to break out of the cowboy mold, and studio big shots agreed in the belief "Red" Barry could be the next James Cagney.

That idea was permanently shelved after complaints from directors and other crew members, whose misfortune it had been to work with the hot-tempered thespian. One contemptuous director called him "The Midget," and another flatly refused to ever make another picture with him.

Given his over-inflated ego, Barry likely thought he was the studio's "hottest property," until the day in 1944 that it showed him the door. But with Roy Rogers, Bill Elliott and Plainview's own Sunset Carson in the Republic stable, he would not be missed.

Feelings could not have been all that hard since Barry returned to Republic Pictures for the occasional curtain call for the rest of the 1940s. In middle age, he learned not to be so picky and accepted any part that came his way in a variety of mostly forgettable films.

But it was television that extended Barry's acting career. He was a natural for guest spots on shows like *The Virginian*, *Little House on the Prairie*, *Maverick*, *Sugarfoot* and other prime-time favorites during the golden age of television Westerns.

In the summer of 1980, police responded to a report of a domestic disturbance at Barry's North Hollywood home. The estranged wife of the sixty-eight-year-old actor had come back to the residence to pick up a few of her things, and that evidently lit her ex-husband's short fuse.

Officers thought they had succeeded in calming everyone down, until Don "Red" Barry suddenly emerged from the house brandishing a .38-caliber revolver. Without saying a word, he fired one round into his head and died in the ambulance on the way to the hospital.

5

# MADGE BELLAMY

## *Silent Film Star Self-Destructed*

Madge Bellamy, future star of the silent screen, was born in Hillsboro in 1900, but the name on the birth certificate read "Margaret Philpott." The talented tyke, whose father coached at the local college, learned to dance before she learned the three Rs.

"I had a stooped way of walking, and the doctor told my parents to send me to dancing school," she said. She appeared in amateur musicals in Denver as a little girl and later as an accomplished adolescent in San Antonio after the family moved back to Texas.

Attracted by the bright lights of the Great White Way, Madge decided to run away from home soon after turning seventeen. She did not go alone to New York City. "My mother said, 'I'll run with you,' so I took her along."

Madge had hardly unpacked her bags when she won a place in the chorus line of a Broadway production entitled *The Love Mill*. Theater owner Daniel Frohman came backstage one evening and announced with convincing confidence that her future was in acting, not dancing. He took his new protégée under his wing and, over her objections, changed her name to Madge Bellamy.

While working on the dramatic stage in New York, Madge made her first motion picture, which was shot in New Jersey. Her 1920 film debut led to a screen test with big-time Hollywood producer Thomas Ince, who immediately signed her to a four-year movie contract.

The ambitious actress hit the ground running in Tinsel Town, with prominent parts in six features in 1921. Her fourth film that busy year was *Hail the Woman,* starring Florence Vidor. "I looked up to her and admired her. She was from Texas, and one would think she had been to the finest finishing schools in Europe."

The breakthrough part for the rising star was the title role in the 1922 version of *Lorna Doone.* The next year, Ince lent his hot property to Mary Pickford for a picture with her brother Jack. "Jack was very sweet to me, and, of course, I was always in love with Mary," Madge stated.

Madge Bellamy in 1943, the year she took three shots at a boyfriend for dumping her. *RGD5F432A, Houston Public Library, HMRC.*

To Ince's dismay, Madge began to show her quirky side. She turned down a major role in the epic *Ben Hur* because she refused to work with horses. The fact that Louis B. Mayer remained seated when she entered his office was reason enough for her to storm out of the room screaming, "I don't want to be in your picture anyway!"

After Thomas Ince's mysterious death in 1924 aboard a yacht owned by publisher William Randolph Hearst, Madge found a new home at Fox Studios. But the relationship was rocky right from the start.

In 1925, the pugnacious prima donna butted heads with director Frank Borzage on the set of *Lazybones.* He got even three years later by choosing Janet Gaynor over Madge for the female lead in the hit *Seventh Heaven.*

Madge had a hot-and-cold love affair with a Fox executive, until she found out he was two-timing her with another actress. She retaliated by eloping to Tijuana with a stockbroker, but her first and only marriage lasted less than a week.

Madge came unglued in 1929 when Fox informed her a first-time director would be in charge of her next picture. She demanded one of her own choosing but was told instead that she could pick her leading man.

That was when Madge self-destructed. She told Fox to tear up her contract and walked off the lot. The studio bosses promised to pay her $25,000 more a year if she would come back, but she said nothing doing.

Madge repeatedly refused to return telephone calls from Fox, while also telling both MGM and Columbia studios to go fly a kite. After a year without a penny of income, she was forced to auction off her home, a copy of a Spanish castle, and her personal belongings.

In dire need of money, Madge returned to Hollywood in 1932. She earned $5,000 for eleven days work in the cult horror film *White Zombie*, with Bela Lugosi.

By 1934, Madge was again under contract to Fox but restricted to low-budget B movies like *Charlie Chan of London*, *Daring Young Man* and *The Great Hotel Murder*. Frustrated and humiliated, she quit for good.

Madge made front-page news in 1943 when she used a wealthy ex-boyfriend for target practice. Determined to make Albert Stanwood Murphy "suffer somehow" for ending their five-year relationship, she stalked him for four days in San Francisco. Spotting her prey getting into his car outside a club, she fired three times but only "winged him."

Madge confessed to shooting at her former lover, but in the next breath claimed, "I had had the little gun so long I thought it was just a toy." The judge took it easy on the faded star, sentencing her to six months probation. She actually came out ahead in the end, when Murphy settled a civil suit out of court by writing her a six-figure check.

After World War II, Madge bought a junkyard in Ontario, California. She avoided the altar like the plague and lived alone the rest of her long life.

Madge Bellamy bared her soul in a telephone interview three months before her death in January 1990. "I'm not very proud of anything," she ruefully admitted. "I had great expectations, but they gave out way before my years gave out. That's too bad, isn't it?"

6

# DAN BLOCKER

## *Television's Lovable Hoss*

If Bobby Don Blocker was not the biggest baby ever born in Bowie County, as relatives swore, the record holder must have been a whopper. The future Hoss began life in 1928 as a fourteen-pound baby.

Blocker stood six feet tall and tipped the scales at two hundred pounds when he entered a San Antonio military academy at age twelve. The boy's prodigious proportions inspired his father to joke, "He's too big to ride and too little to hitch to a wagon."

After the extra-large lad added four more inches and another seventy-five pounds, college football recruiters came knocking on the door. Blocker picked Sul Ross, the state teachers college at Alpine. During his three years of varsity competition, the Lobos did not lose a single game, although they did play Murray State to a 21-21 draw in the Tangerine Bowl on New Year's Day 1949.

Blocker was not, however, the stereotypical jock. As a favor to a girlfriend, he reluctantly appeared in a campus production of *Arsenic and Old Lace* and fell in love with the theater. He switched majors from physical education to drama and directed his own rendition of *Mister Roberts* with a cast composed completely of obliging teammates.

After graduation, Blocker turned down professional football and boxing offers to act in summer stock in Boston. His thespian adventure was interrupted in 1952 when he was drafted into the Korean War.

The infantry sergeant survived the Asian stalemate and, with a Purple Heart, returned to Texas to marry his college sweetheart. For the next few

Dan Blocker in character for hit television show *Bonanza*. *RGD5F3285, Houston Public Library, HMRC.*

years, he taught high school English and drama in Sonora and studied for a master's degree at his alma mater. Electing to pursue a doctorate at UCLA, he moved his family to Southern California in 1956.

Blocker turned to acting to make ends meet and played bit parts in such television horse operas as *Gunsmoke*, *Maverick* and *Cimarron City*. He found steady work as a continuing character on the short-lived *Restless Gun*, starring John Payne, and impressed producer David Dortort with his ability to adapt to any script.

Dortort, whose motto was "entertainment must not be entirely a mirror of life," soon turned to his next small-screen project, a wholesome family Western he called *Bonanza*. He created characters that were "not just drinking, fighting, carousing, shiftless cowboys" but instead epitomized clean-cut virtues like "faith, hope and morality."

*Bonanza* was set in post–Civil War Nevada, where three-time widower Ben Cartwright had staked his claim to a three-thousand-square-mile domain named the Ponderosa. The story line pitted the silver-haired patriarch and his three sons against an endless variety of villains bent on plundering the private paradise.

Producer David Dortort consciously cast the four central characters with specific segments of the viewing public in mind. Father figure Lorne Greene, a former radio announcer once known as the "Voice of Canada," was the ideal choice for Ben. The role of eldest son Adam went to Pernell Roberts, a serious Shakespearean with whom young married men were supposed to identify. Good looks that hopefully would keep young adolescents glued to the tube landed twenty-one-year-old Michael Landon, whose real name was Eugene Maurice Orowitz, the part of Little Joe.

For Hoss, the gentle giant with a heart of gold, Dortort wanted a larger-than-life actor with a natural appeal to "children of all ages." He immediately thought of Blocker, who jumped at the chance to appear in a weekly television program.

*Bonanza* premiered on September 12, 1959, to less than rave reviews. Although Hoss quickly took center stage as the most popular Cartwright due to Blocker's endearing personality and surprising versatility, the show was generally panned by critics. "Another western is just what Saturday night television needs least," wrote the *Variety* reviewer, "and that's what *Bonanza* appears to be—just another western."

But the network gave the much-maligned series, the first Western telecast in color, the opportunity to attract an audience. *Bonanza* broke into the Nielsen Top Twenty in its second season, climbed to second place in its third year and reigned supreme from 1964 through 1967.

The 1965 defection of temperamental Pernell Roberts, the show's harshest critic, had no detrimental effect on the high ratings. But *Bonanza* could not survive the tragic loss of the best-loved member of the Cartwright clan.

The thirteenth season was in the can when Blocker underwent gall bladder surgery in May 1972. The routine operation seemed to go smoothly, but a few hours later, unexpected complications claimed the life of the forty-three-year-old patient.

*Bonanza* was not the same without Hoss, and the network put the show out of its misery halfway through the next season.

However, reruns offer a nostalgic kind of immortality. Dan Blocker lives on in syndication, riding the Ponderosa range and winning the hearts of new generations.

# 7

# LARRY BLYDEN

## *Double Duty on Stage and Small Screen*

Ivan Lawrence Blieden was born into a comfortably middle-class Houston family in 1925. But like so many children of his generation, the "nice Jewish boy" was badly scarred by the Depression.

Times were suddenly tough for the Bliedens after the father, a respected lawyer, lost his job and could not find work for three long years. Little Larry's earliest memories were of "dodging creditors" and the losing battle to make ends meet.

"I assumed that being poor was personal," he reflected in a 1962 interview. "It was hard for me to realize that it was a general condition and not my family's fault."

Unhappy and feeling "personally insignificant," teenaged Larry developed a crippling inferiority complex. Then in high school, he discovered acting and learned "I didn't have to be me. I could be somebody else."

After graduation, Larry did his patriotic duty by serving three years in the Marines. He returned to the Bayou City and earned a degree at the University of Houston, while working part-time as a radio announcer and dabbling in community theater.

With college behind him, Larry decided to devote himself to acting. He studied at the Royal Academy of Arts in London and with the famous Stella Adler in New York.

Changing the spelling and pronunciation of his last name, he landed a few bit parts in Broadway plays before fellow Texan Josh Logan provided his big break—the role of Ensign Frank Pulver in the hit *Mister Roberts.*

Unlike most stage actors, Blyden did not turn up his nose at the new entertainment medium invading America's living rooms in the early 1950s. And with most television programs being produced in New York, he was able to juggle two careers at once.

When Blyden was not on Broadway, he was on television appearing in the weekly dramas so popular at the time. *Playhouse 90*, *The Loretta Young Show*, *Alfred Hitchcock Presents* and a host of others gave the comedian the opportunity to show his serious side.

One of those roles is now considered a classic—that of Rocky Valentine in the *Twilight Zone* episode titled "A Nice Place to Visit," which aired on April 15, 1960. Blyden plays a small-time hoodlum who thinks he has died and gone to heaven because in the afterlife he has everything he ever wanted.

Blyden's charm and quick wit made him a perfect fit for the half-hour game shows that began to catch on with viewers in the 1950s. He was a frequent panelist on *What's My Line?*, *Password* and *To Tell the Truth*.

His growing popularity with the television audience convinced network bosses to try him in his own sitcom. But both *Joe & Mabel* in 1957 and *Harry's Girls* seven years later were summer replacements that did not make it to Labor Day.

In 1955, Blyden married actress, dancer and choreographer Carol Haney. The couple bought a historic house in New Jersey that they came to believe was haunted by the spirit of the builder. Blyden kept the house in their 1962 divorce settlement but sold it soon after his ex-wife's death two years later because the strong aroma of baking brownies, her favorite, convinced him of her ghostly presence.

The only place Blyden did not enjoy at least a measure of success was Hollywood. He appeared in just three films: *Kiss Them for Me* with Gary Grant and Jayne Mansfield in 1957, *The Bachelor Party* with Amarillo's Carolyn Jones and Don Murray that same year and *On a Clear Day You Can See Forever* with Barbra Streisand in 1970. He summed up his short-lived movie career with the wry comment, "The fact that I'm in something sells very few tickets."

Despite his busy television schedule, Blyden's first love was Broadway. In the 1960s alone, he starred with Bert Lahr in the musical *Foxy*, replaced Eli Wallach in the lead role of *Luv*, costarred in the musical *The Apple Tree* and received rave reviews for the comedy *You Know I Can't Hear You When the Water's Running*.

Blyden's game show experience coupled with his ability to work without a script, something very few actors can do, made him an ideal emcee. His first gig as host was on *Personality* in 1967.

Larry Blyden (left) did anything for a laugh, even wear a pith helmet. *RGD5F1125, Houston Public Library, HMRC.*

He soon became, as son Josh put it, "the guy that took over for other guys on game shows." When Bill Leyden suffered a brain hemorrhage, it was Blyden who filled his shoes as the emcee of *You're Putting Me On*. In the case of *The Movie Game*, it was poor ratings that resulted in his replacing the original host. Finally, in 1972, Blyden filled the chair once occupied by the legendary John Charles Daly on *What's My Line?*

In 1972, Blyden took home a Tony, the Broadway equivalent of the Oscar, for his hilarious portrayal of Hysterium the slave in the slapstick comedy *A Funny Thing Happened on the Way to the Forum*.

After *What's My Line?* finally ran out of gas in early 1975, Blyden signed on to host *Showoffs*, with a starting date of June 30. Taking some much-needed time off, he flew to Morocco to hunt for antiques, a favorite pastime of his.

Blyden was badly injured in a one-car accident on May 31, 1975. Although the American consul reported his prognosis was good after emergency surgery, the talented Texan took an unexpected turn for the worse and died five days later at age forty-nine.

That was the official version of the circumstances surrounding Larry Blyden's death. But Barbara Rush, his costar in *What Makes Sammy Run?*, told a very different and disturbing story. The actress said the way she heard it, he was the victim of a carjacking that ended in his murder.

# 8
# FRANK BUCK
## *Brought 'Em Back Alive*

The Texan that grew up to be one of the most recognizable Americans of the 1930s was born in 1884 in Gainesville and raised in Dallas. Fascinated by animals from an early age, Frank Buck was punished by his mother for playing with a copperhead. "Never again let me see you with a snake!" he remembered her warning.

Deciding seven grades of classroom confinement was all the formal education he could stand, Buck dropped out of school. He left home a few years later to ride herd on a cattle train bound for the stockyards of Chicago.

The young Texan stayed in the Windy City and went to work for a local hotel. In 1901, the handsome bellboy married a permanent guest named Amy Leslie, drama critic for the *Chicago Daily News*.

The groom had just turned seventeen, and the bride was forty-six. The May–December marriage lasted more than a decade, nine and a half years longer than anyone would have given it.

One morning in 1911, Buck emerged bleary-eyed from a marathon poker game with $3,500 in winnings. Suddenly, he had the money to do what he always had wanted—travel the world and collect animals. He kissed his soon-to-be ex-wife goodbye and booked passage for Brazil.

Buck was pleasantly surprised to learn that a good living could be made supplying zoos and well-heeled private citizens with unusual creatures from distant lands. And that never-a-dull-moment occupation kept him busy for the next eighteen years.

Frank "Bring 'Em Back Alive" Buck in jungle garb holding tight to a tiger. *RGD5F1205, Houston Public Library, HMRC.*

While he loved animals and hated to see them suffer, Buck was not a wildlife conservationist. It was just that his customers were only willing to pay top dollar for live specimens, not dead ones.

In spite of Buck's best efforts, an alarming number did die in transit. But it was hardly his fault that climate-controlled shipping containers and veterinary antibiotics were years in the future.

On most of his trips, Buck was accompanied by his second wife, Nina. She is remembered for her post-divorce quote: "As long as I live, I don't want to see any animals wilder or bigger than a kitten."

Bad business practices and the stock market crash of 1929 wiped Buck out, leaving him practically penniless. But loans from generous friends helped him pull through and get back on his feet.

Then in 1930, World War I correspondent Floyd Gibbons made a suggestion that changed Buck's life. Why didn't the world traveler put his exciting exploits down on paper?

With the professional assistance of author Edward Anthony, Buck wrote *Bring 'Em Back Alive*. The book was an instant sensation, one that bookstores could not keep in stock. The duo followed their first best seller with a second—*Wild Cargo*.

Frank "Bring 'Em Back Alive" Buck was born, one of the best-known Americans of his day, ranking right up there with Charles Lindbergh, Babe Ruth and Jack Dempsey.

There were more books to come, but Buck was proudest of a grade school reader entitled *On Jungle Trails*. "Wherever I go," he liked to point out, "children mention this book to me and tell me how much they learned about animals and the jungle from it."

With his books selling like hotcakes, the next logical medium was motion pictures. Dressed in his trademark safari attire, Buck starred as himself in the successful screen versions of *Bring 'Em Back Alive* (1932) and *Wild Cargo* (1934).

Other, mostly forgettable, films were *Fang and Claws* (1935), a fifteen-part serial called *Jungle Menace* (1937), *Jungle Cavalcade* (1941), *Jacare* (1942) and *Tiger Fangs* (1943). He scraped the bottom of the barrel in 1949 with *Africa Screams*, also shown under the title *Abbott and Costello in Africa*.

At the peak of his popularity, Buck toured with the Ringling Bros. and Barnum & Bailey Circus. He shook hands with two million people who visited Frank Buck's Jungle Camp at Chicago's A Century of Progress International Exposition in 1933 and brought the exhibit out of mothballs for the 1939 New York World's Fair.

On Buck's first visit to his birthplace in forty-eight years, Gainesville rolled out the red carpet for its famous native son in 1937. The local zoo, one of many he helped stock, was renamed in his honor in 1954.

Buck never recovered completely from injuries sustained in a taxicab wreck in 1947. Hoping to find the cause of his declining health, he underwent a battery of tests in Houston.

The diagnosis was advanced lung cancer. The heavy smoker, who had endorsed cigarettes in newspaper and magazine advertisements, took his last breath not in a faraway jungle but in a hospital bed on March 25, 1950, eight days after his sixty-sixth birthday.

9

# CYD CHARISSE

## "Beautiful Dynamite"

If Tula Ellice Finklea, the name on her birth certificate, does not ring a bell, how about Cyd Charisse, the beautiful brunette who danced her way to stardom in the classic Hollywood musicals of the 1940s and 1950s? She had gone by "Sid" since childhood because that was how her baby brother mispronounced "Sis."

To overcome the effects of a mild case of polio, Sid Finklea's mother and father enrolled their sickly six-year-old in a dance class. By the age of twelve, the gifted girl had learned everything the hired tutors in Amarillo could teach her, so her folks sent her to Los Angeles to study ballet. After only two more years of advanced instruction, the Texas Panhandle prodigy was accepted by the prestigious Ballet Russe de Monte Carlo and began performing under the name Felia Siderova.

In July 1939, the seventeen-year-old Texan up and married her dance instructor Nico Charisse, thirty-two, while on tour in Europe. The next month, Germany invaded Poland in the opening act of the Second World War. The tour was cancelled, the company dissolved and the newlyweds rushed back to the safety of the United States.

A young woman with Sid's looks and talent did not go without work for long in Hollywood. A dancing part in the 1943 movie *Something to Shout About* was followed by similar roles in two other so-so films that same year. But do not look for Sid in the credits. She appeared in all three flicks under the stage alias Lily Norwood.

Those early efforts did not go unnoticed, however. Sid caught the eye of the studio scouts at MGM, reigning monarch of Hollywood musicals, and was soon signed to a long-term contract. MGM started its fresh face off with minor parts in three movies: *The Harvey Girls*, a Judy Garland vehicle that featured Sid's first spoken words, *Till the Clouds Roll By* and *Ziegfeld Follies*, which opened with the newcomer tripping the light fantastic with none other than Fred Astaire.

Prior to its release, *Ziegfeld Follies* producer Arthur Freed changed Sid's name one last time. He took her married name, tinkered with the spelling of her moniker and came up with Cyd Charisse.

That was in 1946. Cyd made ten run-of-the-mill musicals for MGM over the next six years, but her career seemed to be stalled in second gear. All that changed with an historic casting choice for *Singin' in the Rain*.

The movie was already in the can when producer Arthur Freed decided it needed a dream sequence ballet for the finale. Leading man Gene Kelly pushed for his assistant to get the female part, but Freed went with the studio's resident ballerina—Cyd Charisse.

Cyd Charisse (fifth from left) seated next to Glenn McCarthy at the grand opening of the Shamrock Hotel in Houston on St. Patrick's Day 1949. *MSS1248-3747, Houston Public Library, HMRC*

Codirector Stanley Donen later reminisced about the iconic scene: "We needed someone who could stop a man by just sticking up her leg. Cyd was stunning. We stuck a hat on the end of her foot and handed her a cigarette holder. I had to cue her to exhale the cigarette smoke when Gene (Kelly) first runs into her, because she couldn't handle the smoke."

That turned out to be the big break Cyd had been waiting for. A year later, she was cast as the female lead opposite Fred Astaire for *The Band Wagon*. During the filming, Astaire amused the crew by obsessively comparing his slight stature to Cyd's height. Although she was just five feet, six inches tall in her stocking feet, high heels and unusually long legs made her look much taller.

Putting aside his fragile ego, Astaire had nothing but the highest praise for Cyd in his 1959 autobiography *Steps in Time*. He fondly refers to his former partner as "beautiful dynamite" and adds, "That Cyd! When you've danced with her, you stayed danced with."

She returned the compliment in the joint memoir *The Two of Us* written in 1976 with her second husband of sixty years, Tony Martin. "Fred moved like glass," she said simply.

Cyd made three more movies with her two famous partners. She teamed up twice with Gene Kelly for *Brigadoon* in 1954 and *It's Always Fair Weather* two years later and with Astaire for *Silk Stockings* in 1957. Then the curtain came down on the golden age of the Hollywood musical.

Cyd told an interviewer in 2002 that her husband could always tell with which of the two she had been dancing. "If I was black and blue, it was Gene. And if it was Fred, I didn't have a mark on me."

Cyd did not shy away from a critical evaluation of Astaire and Kelly. "As one of the handful of girls who worked with both of those dance geniuses, I think I can give an honest comparison. In my opinion, Kelly is the more inventive choreographer of the two. Astaire…creates fabulous numbers for himself and his partner. But Kelly can create an entire number for somebody else. To sum it up, I'd say they were the two greatest dancing personalities who were ever on screen."

But Cyd Charisse, who passed away in 2008 at the age of eighty-six, has to rank a close third.

10

# VAN CLIBURN

## *Hero in a Tuxedo*

A twenty-three-year-old pianist from Kilgore gave sagging morale back home a badly needed boost by winning first prize at the International Tschaikowsky Competition on April 12, 1958. *Time* magazine celebrated his stunning victory by putting him on the cover under the headline "The Texan Who Conquered Russia."

Van Cliburn was just what the doctor ordered for a country still down in the dumps over the Soviets' Sputnik space spectacular six months earlier. With American morale lower than at any time since Pearl Harbor, the curly headed celebrity was Charles Lindbergh in a tuxedo.

In the rush to claim the superstar as one of their own, Texans tactfully ignored the fact that Harvey Levan Cliburn Jr. was actually born in Shreveport, Louisiana. But his parents soon corrected that "mistake" by moving to the East Texas town of Kilgore and raising their gifted child in the Lone Star State.

Cliburn showed a precocious musical talent at the tender age of three. After nine years of professional instruction from his mother, an accomplished pianist in her own right, he won a contest that resulted in his debut with the Houston Symphony in 1946.

Another prestigious award led to highly acclaimed performances with the New York Philharmonic and the civic orchestras of Cleveland, Buffalo, Denver and Detroit. His phenomenal success opened the door to the world-renown Juilliard School of Music in Manhattan, where he started his studies in 1951.

Famed pianist Liberace (right), an audience of one for fresh-faced Van Cliburn. *Houston Public Library, HMRC.*

During a visit to Juilliard by *Tonight Show* bandleader Skitch Henderson, Cliburn auditioned for the popular program. This chance encounter yielded two guest appearances on national late-night television, which Johnny Carson's bandleader later boasted "kept the kid eating for a year."

By 1957, however, the novelty had worn off for a teenaged prodigy in his early twenties, and a drastic decline in bookings cut his annual income in half. Cliburn was reduced to entertaining the dinner crowd at a Kilgore restaurant in order to pay off a loan at a local bank.

At this critical crossroads in his career, his Juilliard teacher encouraged him to enter the upcoming competition in Moscow. Knowing he would be pitted against the finest young pianists on the planet, he practiced eight hours a day in preparation for the challenge of his life.

The Moscow gold medal in April 1958 came complete with hugs and kisses from Nikita Khruschev, the gruff Soviet strongman better known for his belligerent threat to bury the capitalist West. Although Cold War zealots criticized Cliburn for fraternizing with the communist enemy, he spoke only of his genuine "love affair for the Russian people" and avoided any comment on the Soviet system.

Cliburn's ticker-tape welcome in New York City, the first ever for a musician, was followed by equally ecstatic receptions in Philadelphia, Washington and his native Texas. People who did not know Tschaikowsky from tater tots turned out for a fleeting glimpse of the six-foot-four king of the keyboards.

Before his Moscow magic, Cliburn felt fortunate to earn a hundred dollars a night for tickling the ivories. As a household name, he was now able to command as much as $10,000 a performance. The most amazing proof of his popularity was the unprecedented response to his recording of Tchaikovsky's *Piano Concerto No. 1*, the first classical album to sell a million copies.

But his attempt to satisfy the insatiable appetite of an adoring public did have its down side. When antibiotics failed to cure a chronically sore finger, he had to have the bone surgically scraped. For the next six months, the piano was off-limits.

After more than twenty years of virtually nonstop playing, Cliburn decided to take some time off in 1978. Although he planned on returning to the concert circuit in a year or two, the hard-earned hiatus stretched into a decade, and rumors began to spread that he had become a recluse.

The fifty-three-year-old resident of Fort Worth came out of retirement for a special performance in 1987. Cliburn accepted an invitation from President Ronald Reagan to play at a White House dinner for Russian leader Mikhail Gorbachev.

Anticipating a formal affair, Cliburn presumed he would be shown the door the moment he finished. But after a relaxed conversation with the president, Raisa Gorbachev requested an encore.

"I said I would if she would help me," Cliburn told a Texas newspaper, "and impulsively I sat down and began playing and singing 'Moscow Nights.' After a minute, the Gorbachevs joined in, and we wound up having a sing-along."

Later that night in his hotel room, Cliburn fretted he had gone too far in letting his hair down. "To be honest," he sheepishly confessed, "I was horrified at what I had done."

His mother, always his toughest critic, soothed his fears. He had, after all, started out with classical compositions before going off on the folk music tangent.

Then she added, "But don't you dare do anything like that again!"

Cliburn extended a unique streak by playing the White House one last time in early 2012. He had treated every president from Truman to Obama to a private recital.

Cliburn was a lifelong night owl. He would practice until five o'clock in the morning and sleep until well after noon. "You feel like you're alone and the world is asleep. It's very inspiring."

The world learned in the summer of 2012 that Van Cliburn had terminal bone cancer. Less than a year later, he died at his Fort Worth residence at the age of seventy-eight.

11

# JOAN CRAWFORD

## *Self-Made Movie Star*

Life was an uphill struggle from the very start for Lucille Fay LeSueur, born in San Antonio in either 1904, 1905 or 1906. Her father abandoned the family while she was still in the womb, leaving her mother in desperately dire straits.

Shortly after giving birth, Anna LeSueur moved with her newborn and a son, who was not much older than his baby sister, to Lawton, Oklahoma, where she had friends and kinfolk. She met and soon married Henry Cassin, owner of a local theater called the Ramsey Opera House.

Despite the name, vaudeville was Cassin's bread and butter. Lucille watched the endless parade of acts from backstage, paying particular attention to the dancers. Encouraged by her stepfather, she began dancing herself during the brief intermissions.

Even though Cassin beat the case in court, the scandal from an embezzlement charge caused the family to relocate to Kansas City. "Billie," as she was called, was in her teens when her parents separated. Forced to do the cooking, cleaning and other household chores, she stopped going to school altogether, ending up with only an elementary education.

Around the time she turned eighteen, Billie left home to chase her childhood dream of becoming a professional dancer. Taking back her birth name of Lucille LeSueur, she joined the chorus line of a traveling revue.

Producer Jacob J. Shubert happened to be in the audience the night the troupe opened in Detroit. He hired Lucille on the spot for his Broadway show

*Innocent Eyes*, and the next week, she was tripping the light fantastic in New York City.

Everything continued to fall almost magically into place for Lucille. The publicist for the Loews Theater chain arranged a screen test with MGM. She was spending Christmas at her mother's place in Kansas City when the telegram came with the studio's offer of a seventy-five-dollars-a-week contract. Excited beyond words, she borrowed the money for a train ticket to California and reported for work on New Year's Day 1925.

The intensity that drove her stardom is as plain as day in this image of Joan Crawford. *RGD5-B002-F031A-832, Houston Public Library, HMRC.*

MGM kept its new hire busy, to say the least. In her first year on the payroll, Lucille appeared in no fewer than thirteen films, all silent of course. Every part was anonymous, meaning her name was omitted from the credits.

But the head of publicity at MGM saw Lucille's star potential, an opinion he shared with studio boss Louis B. Mayer. Both agreed she needed a new name—LeSueur sounded too much like "sewer"—and prevailed upon a fan magazine to sponsor a contest.

The winning name was "Joan Arden," but that turned out to be the real name of an extra on the MGM lot. So they settled on the runner-up, "Joan Crawford," which the actress never liked because it reminded her of crawfish.

Crawford was not one to sit back and wait for the studio to give her top billing. Understanding the importance of being seen while showcasing her original talent, she attended the dances held at the Hollywood hotels and frequently won the Charleston and Black Bottom competitions.

On her rise up the ranks of MGM's contract players, a former scriptwriter once commented, "No one decided to make Joan Crawford a star. Joan Crawford became a star because Joan Crawford decided to become a star."

Her parts got better and bigger, leading to Crawford's selection as one of the "Baby Stars" of 1926. She was in impressive company with Fay Wray, Dolores del Rio, Janet Gaynor and Mary Astor on the list of female up-and-comers.

In 1927, Crawford was cast as the assistant to Lon Chaney Sr. in *The Unknown*, a silent classic about an armless knife thrower. Years later, she claimed to have learned more about acting from Chaney than anybody else in her entire career.

Crawford's high energy and rather risqué performance in the 1928 hit *Our Dancing Daughters* vaulted her to stardom. No less than F. Scott Fitzgerald wrote, "Joan Crawford is doubtless the best example of the flapper."

As a symbol of her admission into Hollywood "high society," Crawford wed Douglas Fairbanks Jr. in 1928. Fairbanks Sr. and his wife, Mary Pickford, were opposed to the marriage, refusing for months to allow the bride even to set foot in their mansion, but she proved how good an actress she really was by eventually winning over her in-laws.

While most stars of the silent era never successfully switched to "talkies," Crawford hit her stride with sound. Behind the scenes, she toiled tirelessly to rid herself of the slightest trace of her Texan/Okie accent.

"I would lock myself in my room and read newspapers, magazines and books aloud. At my elbow I kept a dictionary. When I came to a word I did not know how to pronounce, I looked it up and repeated it correctly 15 times."

She was a box-office queen during the Depression and the Second World War, and the peak of her long career came at the 1945 Academy Awards ceremony. Crawford took home the Best Actress Oscar for her sixty-eighth motion picture, *Mildred Pierce.*

In middle age, Crawford had to fight for the choice parts usually reserved for younger actresses. But fight she did until the final curtain came down in 1977.

In her will, Crawford left identical dollar amounts to her two youngest children, Cindy and Cathy, but had this to say about her two oldest: "It is my intention to make no provision herein for my son, Christopher, or my daughter, Christina, for reasons which are well known to them."

Christina retaliated by dragging her dead mother's memory through the mud in the scathing tell-all book *Mommie Dearest,* published the year after Crawford's death. Many old friends and coworkers, including Myrna Loy, Katherine Hepburn, Ann Blyth and ex-husband Douglas Fairbanks Jr., came to Crawford's public defense and denied ever witnessing the emotional and physical abuse Christina claimed.

Nevertheless, the best seller and the movie of the same name, starring Faye Dunaway, did irreparable damage to the legacy of one of Hollywood's brightest stars.

# 12
# LINDA DARNELL
## *A Life and Career Up in Flames*

The headline put on Sheilah Graham's gossip column in the *Dallas Morning News* for July 25, 1939, read: "New Screen Romance Involves Our Linda." It focused more on the real age of the young actress than her love life.

Born in Dallas in 1923, Monetta Eloyse Darnell grew up in Oak Cliff and attended Sunset High School. Her mother was bound and determined to see one of her three daughters on the silver screen, and "Tweedles"—a family nickname—drew the short straw.

Pearl Darnell had her little darling tap dancing at four and seven years later pushed her into modeling for a Dallas department store. By age thirteen, Tweedles had appeared in local theater productions and landed a job as a hostess or "Texanita" at the Lone Star Centennial.

The fourteen-year-old entered a *Gateway to Hollywood* contest with a backdated birthday and finished first in the Southwest region. As a consolation prize for her loss in the final round, she was given a screen test by RKO. The moviemakers liked what they saw but not enough to put the fresh face on the payroll.

Tweedles never forgot her less-than-triumphant return to Dallas. "It was hell to go home and have everybody ask how you were making out in Hollywood. I was just miserable."

But a Twentieth Century Fox talent scout remembered the beautiful brunette and in April 1939 persuaded studio executives to bring her back to Tinsel Town. The studio changed her name to Linda, bumped her age up

This 1944 photograph shows why twenty-one-year-old Linda Darnell was considered one of the most beautiful actresses in motion pictures. *RGD5F4450, Houston Public Library, HMRC.*

to eighteen and signed her to a seven-year contract with a starting salary of seventy-five dollars per week.

Within the month and without any training, the inexperienced adolescent went in front of the camera. *Hotel for Women* was a very inauspicious debut, and her second film was not much better. Linda's costar in the romantic comedy *Day-Time Wife* was matinee idol Tyrone Power, with whom she made three more pictures (*Brigham Young*, *The Mark of Zorro* and *Blood and Sand*) in a year and a half.

Twentieth Century Fox rewarded the hardworking starlet with a hefty pay raise that increased her weekly income tenfold. But her meddling mother maintained tight control of the minor's money and managed to funnel more than $100,000 into a "trust fund."

Linda never adjusted to life in Hollywood. She reportedly made only one close friend, Texan Ann Miller, possibly because the two launched their careers at such an early age. As for the film industry's social scene, Linda used a single word to describe it—"nauseating."

In an interview with her biographer given in middle age, Linda talked about what it was like to be a naïve teen actress:

> *At first, everything was like a fairy tale come true. I stepped into a fabulous land where, overnight, I was a movie star. In pictures you're built up by everyone. On the set, in the publicity office, wherever you go, everyone says you're wonderful.*
>
> *It gives you a false sense of security. You waltz through a role, and everywhere you hear that you are beautiful and lovely, a natural-born actress. You believe what people around you say.*

Linda left home in 1942 and eloped the following April with the cameraman, who shot her screen test and first three flicks. The twice divorced groom was forty-two, twenty-three years older than the bride.

In 1944, the year *Look* magazine chose her as one of the four most beautiful women in Hollywood, Linda appeared in her fourteenth film. The tight blouse and short skirt she wore in *Summer Storm* turned the "sweet young thing" into a "sultry vixen," resulting in mature roles that required more than merely looking pretty.

Linda played a music hall Jezebel strangled by an insane lover in *Hanover Square* (1945) and a seductive waitress who met an almost identical fate in *Fallen Angel*, also released at the end of the war. The year 1946 featured two more doomed characters: a concubine burned at the stake (*Anna and the King of Siam*) and a saloon singer shot to death (*My Darling Clementine*).

The title role in *Forever Amber*, the costume epic that should have vaulted her into the big time, backfired on Linda. Critics crucified her for sleepwalking through the $3 million box-office flop, and Fox blamed her for disappointing ticket sales.

Linda kept plugging away in low-budget tearjerkers like *The Walls of Jericho*, *A Letter to Three Wives* and *Wife, Husband, Friend*. Then came her highly acclaimed performance in the 1950 film *No Way Out*, which according to a rave review in *Look* "raises her to a position as one of the screen's top dramatic actresses."

But in 1952, right after the breakup of her eight-year marriage, Fox let Linda go in order to devote its undivided attention to newcomer Marilyn Monroe. Parts were scarce for a homeless actress in her forties, and she made only eight more movies—none worth mentioning.

Neither were her second and third rides on the marital merry-go-round. Linda's marriage to a beer heir lasted less than two years, and an obscure pilot sued for divorce after five.

In 1956, Linda tried her luck on Broadway in *Harbor Lights*, but the producers pulled the plug on the fourth night. She fared better on television in shows like *Screen Directors Playhouse*, *Climax*, *Wagon Train*, *Playhouse 90* and the *Jane Wyman Theater* but failed to get her own series on the air.

On the evening of April 9, 1965, Linda took a nostalgic walk down memory lane with her former secretary. They reminisced about the good old days in Hollywood and watched one of the Texas actress's early movies on television.

Linda Darnell's hopes of a comeback went up in flames later that night. Firemen rescued her ex-secretary and the woman's daughter from the blazing townhouse, but their famous guest suffered burns over eighty percent of her body and died the next day in a Chicago hospital.

# 13
# JIMMY DEAN
## *More than a Sausage Salesman*

Jimmy Ray Dean was born in Plainview the summer before the stock market crashed. His father's answer to the Depression was to run off, leaving his wife to raise their two boys all by herself during the hardest times in living memory.

Too proud to accept New Deal relief, Ruth Dean turned sugar sacks into shirts for her sons. The other kids never tired of making fun of Jimmy's scarecrow appearance, but he credited the constant ridicule with lighting the fire of a burning ambition.

Even as a six-year-old, Dean had to do his part to put food on the table. "I was a hard working little boy," he told a *TV Guide* interviewer in 1964. "Oh, I worked. Pulling cotton, shocking grain, cutting wheat, loading wheat, chopping cotton, cleaning chicken houses, milking cows, plowing."

Besides an uncompromising work ethic, Dean's mother also instilled a love of music and even taught him to play the piano. He later learned the harmonica, accordion and guitar on his own.

Dean dropped out of high school at sixteen to help support the hard-pressed family but wound up joining the Merchant Marines and later the Air Force. It was while he was stationed at an air base near Washington, D.C., that he got his first paying gig as a musician by filling in with his accordion for a sick fiddle player.

After his discharge, Dean remained in the Washington area, forming one short-lived musical group, the Tennessee Haymakers, before the Texas Wildcats came about in 1952. The next year, he recorded his one and only hit single of the decade, "Bummin' Around."

However, Dean and the Texas Wildcats found the success that eluded them in the recording studio with a radio show called *Town and Country Time*. The Texan and his backup band, which included Roy Clark until Dean fired him for being late once too often, attracted loyal listeners in Delaware, Maryland and Virginia as well as metropolitan D.C.

In 1957, the Wildcats and their personable front man parlayed their popularity into a three-hour, Saturday night television program billed as *Town and Country Jamboree*. That same year, Dean proved he could fly solo as the host of a weekday morning show.

Impressed by the talented Texan's down-home demeanor and sense of humor, CBS picked up *Country Style* under the name *The Morning Show* for its local affiliates. For eight months, the country boy from the Texas Panhandle gave Dave Garroway and the well-established *Today Show* a run for their money.

The end of *The Morning Show* did not mean Dean's television career was over. Within the year, he was back on CBS with *The Jimmy Dean Show*, which aired six afternoons a week until June 1959.

Dean may not have been on the small screen in 1961, but his voice seemed to be on the radio twenty-four hours a day. "Big Bad John," the talking ballad about a self-sacrificing miner that Dean wrote on an airplane in an hour and a half, skyrocketed to the top of the pop music chart and stayed there for five weeks. The biggest hit of his career sold more than a million copies and won him a Grammy for Best Country and Western Recording.

By 1963, Dean was back in America's living room with a weekly variety show that helped to bring country music into the cultural mainstream. It was on *The Jimmy Dean Show* that Roger Miller introduced "King of the Road." The appreciative performer sent his fellow Texan a gold doorknob mounted on a piece of mahogany with the inscription: "To Jimmy Dean. For the one million doors you've opened for me, I'm forever grateful."

Although *The Jimmy Dean Show* was cancelled after three years, its namesake was no stranger to television. He was an occasional guest on programs like *The Ed Sullivan Show*, *The Pat Boone Chevy Showroom* and *The Hollywood Palace*.

Dean also tried his luck at acting. He appeared in six episodes of Fess Parker's television series *Daniel Boone*, along with *Fantasy Island* and other prime time programs. In 1971, he landed a major part in the James Bond movie *Diamonds Are Forever* as an eccentric millionaire easily mistaken for Howard Hughes.

Jimmy Dean in a gag shot with actress Jackie Hayes. *RGD5F1009, Houston Public Library, HMRC.*

Two years earlier, Dean had gotten into the sausage-making business, with a Plainview plant run by his brother. His appealing off-the-cuff commercials made Jimmy Dean Sausage a hot item in grocery stores, and he stayed on as spokesman for the breakfast food after selling the company to Sara Lee in 1984.

Late in life, Dean returned to his roots. Plainview honored him with a "Jimmy Dean Day" and the high school presented him with a treasured diploma. Dean and his wife donated $1 million to Wayland Baptist University in 2008, a record-breaking check for a small college with an enrollment of twelve hundred.

Not many celebrities poke fun at themselves when choosing a title for their autobiography. But for Dean, it came as no surprise that he called his 2004 life story *30 Years of Sausage, 50 Years of Ham.*

Two summers later, in June 2010, Jimmy Dean passed while away watching television in his Virginia home. He is entombed on the grounds in a nine-foot-high, piano-shaped mausoleum that bears an epitaph borrowed from the last line of "Big Bad John"—"Here Lies One Hell of a Man."

14

# J. FRANK DOBIE

## "Mister Texas"

The future folklorist was born in 1888 on the family ranch south of San Antonio. The closest community was six miles away, the Live Oak County village of Dinero.

To some, the Brush Country of his birth and upbringing was a bleak wasteland, but not to James Frank Dobie. For him, it was love at first sight, a passionate bond that caused his mother to remark, "Why, son, you think more of the ranch than of your own people."

Daddy Dobie, a strict fundamentalist, read to his six children from the Bible, while their mother nurtured them on a long list of classics that included *Ivanhoe*, *Pilgrim's Progress*, *Robinson Crusoe* and *David Copperfield*.

Despite their differences, both parents emphasized education. They hired a governess to teach Dobie and his nearest sibling until a schoolhouse was built on the ranch. Then at age sixteen, he was sent to Alice to live with grandparents and to attend high school.

Two years later, Dobie enrolled at Southwestern University in Georgetown. He held his own in class, but the size of the place—six hundred students!—overwhelmed him.

By his junior year, the shy youth had come out of his shell. He was on the staff of the student newspaper, a cheerleader for the baseball team and a regular contributor to the literary magazine. He also found his first cause, an anti-elitist crusade against fraternities and sororities. Always the champion of the underdog, he admitted years later, "I cannot remember when I was not on the side of rebels."

J. Frank Dobie in his study surrounded by the animal trophies of a lifetime. *RGD5F623a, Houston Public Library, HMRC.*

After graduation in the spring of 1910, Dobie got his first teaching job at faraway Alpine. He returned to Southwestern the following year, where he taught until going to New York City in 1913 for postgraduate study at Columbia.

His master's degree landed Dobie a faculty position at the University of Texas (UT) in 1914. He was not altogether happy with his colleagues and complained to his mother that he preferred the company of down-to-earth cattlemen over pretentious professors. "Law me!" she snorted in disbelief. "Some of them don't have brains enough to fry an egg in!"

After a six-year courtship conducted almost exclusively by correspondence, Dobie married Bertha McKee, whom he had met at Southwestern. Eight months later, he left his sickly bride to fight "the war to end all wars." He was discharged in time for the fall 1919 semester at UT but resigned before the spring term to lend his favorite uncle a hand.

Dobie's year on the Rancho de Los Olmos proved to be the turning point of his life. He returned to Austin in 1921 with a calling—to collect the stories Texans passed down by word-of-mouth and to transform the tales into literature.

Meanwhile, Dobie's rocky relationship with the UT establishment went from bad to worse. The vast majority of faculty members, born and educated out of state, looked down their noses at Texas. For example, when the token Texan suggested a course on Southwestern literature, they informed him there was no such thing.

After Dobie was told he could not expect to advance up the academic ladder without a doctorate, the situation came to a head. Refusing on principle to satisfy the requirement, he bolted to Oklahoma State and did not come back until friends negotiated a modest raise and a face-saving promotion.

The publication of *A Vaquero of the Brush Country* in 1931 established the maverick "as a spokesman of Texas southwestern culture." But the spectacular success two years later of *Coronado's Children* forever changed Dobie's life and earned the grudging respect of his snobbish peers. In 1933, he was promoted to full professor—a first for a native Texan and an instructor without the obligatory doctoral degree.

The 1930s was a prolific decade for Dobie. He published *On the Open Range*, *Tales of the Mustang*, *The Flavor of Texas* and *Apache Gold and Yanqui Silver* and in 1939 started a weekly newspaper column that he wrote until his death.

Dobie's dogged defense of embattled UT president Homer P. Rainey, along with his outspoken advocacy of unions' right to strike during World War II and full voting rights for blacks, resulted in his dismissal by the board of regents. Finally freed to write full-time, he produced *The Voice of the Coyotes* (1949), *The Ben Lilly Legend* (1950), *The Mustangs* (1952), *Tales of Old Time Texas* (1955), *Up the Trail from Texas* (1955) and *I'll Tell You a Tale* (1960).

"Mister Texas" was never his same energetic self after a bad bout with pneumonia in 1957. Five years later, he was seriously injured in a car wreck near his Austin home, and only an emergency tracheotomy kept him aboveground.

The week before his seventy-sixth birthday in 1964, Dobie received the first copy of *Cow People* in the morning mail. Later that day, he lay down for his afternoon siesta and never woke up.

"The important thing in life is to see clearly," J. Frank Dobie once advised a young admirer. "See all you can. And above all, live by what you, yourself, see."

15

# ALLEN DRURY

## *Best-Selling First Novel*

An August 1959 book review had nothing but the highest praise for a newspaperman's first novel: "It may be a long time before a better one comes along."

Allen Stuart Drury was born in Houston during the First World War and grew up in a small California town. After earning his degree in journalism from Stanford, the cub reporter's first job was on a weekly paper, where in 1940 he won a national award for editorial writing.

Following military service in World War II, Drury moved to Washington, D.C. During the next decade, he covered Capitol Hill for United Press, *Pathfinder Magazine* and the *Washington Evening Star* before joining the Washington bureau of the *New York Times* in 1954.

For seven long years, Drury worked in secret on an epic tale. Then one day in 1958, he shoved a cardboard box containing the first draft into the hands of a fellow *Times* staffer with the modest announcement: "I've written a novel."

"I groaned silently," Russell Baker remembered many years later. "I took it home, ate, fixed a drink, sat down and with a heavy heart reached into this box for a fistful of manuscript. Good Lord! You couldn't put the thing down!"

The newspaperman took readers on a 616-page magical mystery tour of Cold War Washington, giving them a behind-the-scenes peek at politics in the raw. For his title, he appropriated a phrase from a sentence in the Constitution: "The Senate shall advise and consent to the president's nominations to the cabinet."

Unlike other novels with a Washington setting written before and since, *Advise and Consent* was not a fictionalized version of actual events. Drury, who took life and politics very seriously, used a plausible plot and believable characters to explore issues with staying power and to put human nature under the microscope.

Here is *Advise and Consent* in a nutshell: The president nominates Robert A. Leffingwell, a polished but arrogant liberal, as secretary of state, much to the dismay of an old Southern senator from the conservative wing of his own party. Convinced Leffingwell is soft on the Soviets, if not a subversive himself, Senator Seabright Cooley moves heaven and earth to block his confirmation by the U.S. Senate.

When Brigham Anderson, an idealistic young senator from Utah, makes up his mind to cast the decisive vote against Leffingwell, a columnist digs up a hidden homosexual encounter from his past. Anderson cannot live with the scandal and commits suicide.

Drury did not let his high opinion of the Senate as an institution stand in the way of exposing cynicism in the cloakroom. In a revealing exchange that pulls back the curtain, the majority leader tells the head of the opposition, "I'll have to give the papers a statement charging an unprincipled, underhanded coalition against the people's interests, you know." "Go ahead," the second senator says with a shrug. "We've all survived that one before."

Like a man who still eats sausage after seeing it made, Drury loved Washington, warts and all. "It is a city of temporaries, a city of just-arriveds and only-visitings, built on the shifting sands of politics, filled with people passing through. They go home…but hurry back to their lodestones and their star, their self-hypnotized, self-mesmerized, self-enamored, self-propelling, wonderful city they cannot live away from or live without," he said.

The phenomenal success of *Advise and Consent* was due in part to perfect timing—it happened to hit bookstores during the presidential campaign of 1960, which revived public interest in the political process. A priceless piece of free publicity was a photograph of candidates Kennedy and Nixon looking at a copy together.

*Advise and Consent* stayed on the *New York Times* best-seller list for a record 102 weeks and won the Pulitzer Prize for Fiction. It was made into a Broadway play and a motion picture, directed by Otto Preminger and starring Henry Fonda as Leffingwell, Charles Laughton as Senator Cooley and Don Murray as Senator Anderson.

The Capitol was the ideal backdrop for Alan Drury, whose political novel *Advise and Consent* was flying off bookshelves in 1959. *RGD5F7003, Houston Public Library, HMRC.*

Drury quit the *Times* and never worked another day for a newspaper. He became political correspondent for *Reader's Digest*, a high-profile position that provided a steady income, and went right to work on his next novel.

In 1964, Drury bought a house with a breathtaking view of San Francisco Bay. The early riser wrote in the mornings and spent his afternoons researching and editing.

A bachelor who lived alone his entire life, Drury put a premium on privacy. According to a nephew, one of the few people ever to get close to him, "Quality time with Al meant you read your book while he read his."

Allen Drury wrote eighteen more novels as well as five works of nonfiction on subjects as diverse as ancient Egypt and the Nixon White House. But none could hold a candle to his first book. In 1995, three years before the author died on his eightieth birthday, Speaker of the House Newt Gingrich included *Advise and Consent* on a must-read list for new Republican congressmen.

16

# BOBBY FULLER

## *Puzzling Death of Rock Sensation*

On the afternoon of July 15, 1966, Bobby Fuller's mother noticed her Oldsmobile parked in front of the Hollywood apartment she shared with the young singing sensation. The worried woman hurried outside, jerked open the car door and there on the front seat was her boy's bruised and battered body.

Before Goose Creek was gobbled up by Baytown, the Harris County community was the birthplace of two famous entertainers. Legendary singer Bobby Fuller was born in October 1943 followed eight months later by actor Gary Busey.

When Fuller was fourteen, his family went as far west as possible without leaving Texas. Soon after settling in El Paso, the teenaged drummer formed a band he called the Counts and played in shopping center parking lots around town.

The gifted musician graduated from Ysleta High School in 1960 and within two years created the Bobby Fuller Four. The namesake moved up to the microphone as lead singer, delegating the drumming duties to Dalton Powell. The two guitarists were Jim Reese on rhythm and Fuller's brother Randy on bass.

Although quiet and reserved by nature, the handsome vocalist was a charismatic ball of fire onstage. The first disc jockey to give Fuller's records air time still marvels at his "incredible presence….Once he came on, you couldn't take your eyes off him."

Fuller built a recording studio and released "I Fought the Law" on his own label. On the strength of this regional hit, he billed himself as "The Rock and Roll King of the Southwest," no idle boast since Lubbock native Buddy Holly had perished four years earlier in a plane crash. He also opened the Teen Rendezvous Club, a popular place with the underage set before it burned to the ground in 1964.

Rather than rebuild the nightspot, Fuller decided the time had come for The Four to try their luck in California. Randy Fuller and Jim Reese were raring to go, but Dalton Powell refused to quit his day job and passed the drums on to Dewayne Querico.

The band moved to Los Angeles, where promoter Bob Keane, of Del-Fi Records, took the Texas quartet under his experienced wing. The Four attracted national attention with "Let Her Dance," but it was their fabulous follow-up that carried them to the top of the charts. "I Fought the Law," new to the rest of the country, became Bobby Fuller's signature song and an adolescent anthem that has never gone out of style.

After Fuller made his movie debut in the swimsuit saga *Bikini Party in a Haunted House*, The Four went on the road for two cross-country tours. On the surface, they were living the dream, but behind the scenes, there was trouble in paradise.

Fuller and Keane fought like cats and dogs over the musical direction of the band and where all the money was going. By the time the tired troubadours finally trudged back to the Sunshine State, their leader had plans for a solo career.

The telephone woke Fuller up from a deep sleep at three o'clock in the morning on a July night in 1966. He hung up after a brief conversation and said on his way out the door, "Mama, I'll be back."

Bobby Fuller's dead body was sprawled across the front seat of the Oldsmobile. His hair and clothes were wet with gasoline, apparently from the open can on the floorboard. His swollen face, bruised chest and shoulders, twisted right arm and fractured right index finger strongly suggested a vicious beating.

Boyd Elder, a friend who arrived soon after the body was discovered, bitterly complained that the police "didn't seal the scene off, didn't use police tape, didn't take fingerprints, didn't look for evidence, didn't do a thing except say, 'Get the hell out of here.' "

Bob Keane swore to his dying day that a policeman removed the gas can from the car and tossed it in the trash. "Hey, that's evidence," he objected. "How do we know he wasn't killed?"

But the Los Angeles Police Department, with its long history of botched investigations, ruled out murder right from the start. Ignoring the obvious signs of foul play, detectives insisted the singer had committed suicide.

No one who knew the rising star bought that story. "He was on the verge of major success," Casey Kaseem recalled years later. "I would never believe that he took his own life."

The coroner waited two months before announcing the official cause of death—accidental asphyxiation from sniffing gasoline. According to rumors that refuse to die, the verdict was worth a cool million to the executives at Del-Fi, who reportedly had taken out a seven-figure life insurance policy on its hot property.

"My brother once told me," Randy Fuller later reminisced during a televised interview, "it's funny how when somebody dies their music becomes more popular." But there is nothing funny about the sinister circumstances surrounding Bobby Fuller's mysterious demise.

17

# FRED GIPSON

## *Old Yeller Author*

Frederick Benjamin Gipson was born on a farm near Mason in 1908. Life on the western edge of the Hill Country was more hardscrabble than idyllic, but to the young boy, it was a rustic paradise that made a deep and lasting impression.

Gipson was in the tenth grade when he saw his written words in print for the first time. A short story about two lads who tracked down a cattle rustler was the sophomore's modest contribution to *The Branding Iron*, the Mason High School yearbook. He did not consider it an especially noteworthy achievement, but his classmates and teachers sure did.

While the teenager enjoyed all the attention, it did not ignite a burning desire to become a writer or even an interest in higher education. He watched the more ambitious members of the class of 1926 go off to college but chose to stay put after a bookkeeping course in San Antonio soured him on schooling.

After seven years of working odd outdoor jobs in the sweltering heat and freezing cold, Gipson decided to tag along when his younger brother left for the University of Texas (UT). In the "big" city of Austin surrounded by a sea of younger faces, he felt like a fish out of water—until he found his place in the journalism department.

Gipson had his freshman English professor to thank for that. The instructor recognized raw talent when he saw it and regularly read the older student's essays and stories to the class. It was at his urging that Gipson switched to journalism and joined the staff of the campus newspaper, the *Daily Texan*.

*Old Yeller* author Fred Gipson not only loved writing about dogs but also loved having his own canine companions around. *T810.9G44C-P.101, Houston Public Library, HMRC.*

Over the next three years, Gipson blossomed into the shining star of the UT journalism department. He wrote a popular column called One Thing and Then Another that ran on the editorial page of the *Daily Texan*, and one of his folksy fiction pieces appeared in *Southwest Review*, the literary quarterly published by Southern Methodist University, which rewarded him with the princely sum of ten dollars.

If Gipson had hung around the university for another semester or two, he could have departed with diploma in hand. But there was a job waiting for him at the *Caller-Times* in Corpus Christi, where the publisher happened to be a big fan. Following a farewell dinner attended by his many friends and admirers, he left Austin for the Gulf Coast in the winter of 1937.

Instead of starting as a cub reporter chained to a desk, Gipson roamed the countryside writing about whatever he wanted. The dream assignment was right up his alley, and within months, the "roving" columnist had a large and enthusiastic readership.

During his travels, Gipson met a high school senior in San Angelo by the name of Tommie Wynn. Despite the fourteen-year difference in their ages, they married with the blessing of the bride's parents in January 1940.

Gipson had no sooner combed the wedding confetti out of his hair than he was out of work. His benefactor at the *Caller-Times* had died, and the new publisher insisted the gypsy journalist punch a clock like everyone else—and for less money. He objected to the cut in pay and was fired on the spot.

Gipson moved back to Mason with a pregnant wife and no prospects. For as long as he could remember, he had toyed with the idea of earning a living as a freelance writer. The time had come to make that dream a reality.

Six lean years and two children later, the struggling author published his first full-length book, *The Fabulous Empire: Colonel Zack Miller's Story*. The editor of *Southwest Review* had given Gipson the idea for a biography of the colorful Wild West showman and even talked Miller into letting the unknown Texan write his life story.

Sales of *The Fabulous Empire* were respectable, but it was *Hound-Dog Man* three years later that put Gipson on the literary map. The book-of-the-month selection sold more than a quarter of a million copies in its initial twelve months in print.

With the wolf forever banished from his door, Gipson was freed to focus on what he did best—write. The result was five books in as many years: *The Home Place* (1950), *Big Bend: A Homesteader's Story* (1952), *Cowhand: The Story of a Working Cowboy* (1953), *The Trail-Driving Rooster* (1955) and *Recollection Creek* (1955).

In Gipson's eyes, the book that came out in 1956 was his best, and the public concurred. *Old Yeller* flew off bookshelves to the tune of three million copies in the celebrated creator's lifetime, and Walt Disney paid the Hill Country storyteller a king's ransom for the privilege of turning the sentimental saga into a big-screen classic.

Fred Gipson had only one more book left in him, the sequel to *Old Yeller*, entitled *Savage Sam*, which was also made into a Disney movie. It was success not poverty that got the better of him, as drinking, drugs and chronic depression ruined his career and personal life prior to his death in 1973 from a cerebral hemorrhage.

18

# CORINNE GRIFFITH

## "The Orchid Lady"

Every seat was full in Dallas's Crystal Theater for every showing of *The Girl of Today* on September 30, 1918, because Corinne Griffith was there in person to promote her latest silent picture. Just three years earlier in November 1915, the *Morning News* informed readers: "Texarkana has given to the world who it is claimed will be a real star of the movies in the person of Miss Corinne Griffin (stage name Griffith)."

Born in 1895, Corinne, the daughter of a Methodist minister, lived in the town that straddles the Texas-Arkansas border until she was ten. Her mother then took her to a finishing school in New Orleans, where the teenager dazzled everybody, including the judges of a Mardis Gras beauty contest, with her grace and stunning good looks.

There are two versions of how Corinne got her big break. In the first, a Vitagraph director spied her at a high-society function in the Crescent City and offered her a movie contract on the spot. In the second, Texas-born director King Vidor opened the door to her silent-screen debut at age twenty.

Corinne started out as a bit player in so-called two-reelers with a Western theme. But Vitagraph bosses soon realized they had a hot property on their hands and began casting her as the leading lady in their feature films.

After only two years in front of the camera, Corinne was receiving top billing in expensive productions custom-made for her. To quote a historian of the silent era, "Griffith played a series of beautiful yet suffering women in dramas whose focal points became the star's ever-changing wardrobe. She made up for a lack of thespian talent by sheer beauty."

Corinne Griffith turned the tidy sum she made in silent movies into a $150 million fortune by time she died in 1979. *RGD5B001F0024573, Houston Public Library, HMRC.*

Fans and Hollywood types as well were often at a loss for words to describe the beauty of the "Orchid Lady," a studio-invented nickname, but not Adele Rogers St. Johns, queen of the fan magazines. She wrote in 1923: "Her physical charms are too obvious to mention. In the old days, her little, slender feet, and her lovely hands—have you ever noticed her hands?—and her white teeth and her soft hair would have been the subject of poems."

Although she could have skated by on her physical assets alone, Corinne took a serious interest in all phases of moviemaking. After putting in ten or twelve hours on the set, she did not party all night like most actresses of those wild times but spent her evenings instead at the studio watching the "daily rushes," reviewing scripts, making cast suggestions and learning the finer points of behind-the-scenes production.

An important part of the Griffith persona that made her so popular with the public was her pure-as-the-driven-snow reputation. She did not smoke, curse or even wear makeup off camera, a puritanical code of conduct that caused St. Johns to comment, "She is innocence personified." Clean living clearly helped her weather the scandalous storms that would have damaged or destroyed the career of most twice-divorced actresses.

Sadly, Corinne was one of the famous casualties of the "talkies." She tried to make the transition from silent pictures but simply did not have the voice. In a review of *Lilies of the Field*, a 1930 flick with sound segments, *Time* magazine pointed out, "Pretty Corinne Griffith talks through her nose in her first sound film."

In no time at all, the "Orchid Lady" went from box-office gold to box-office poison. First National, Corinne's employer for the past seven years, agreed to pay her off if she would just leave quietly. She accepted their generous terms with the parting words, "Why should I go on until I am playing mother roles? I have plenty of money."

That was no exaggeration. At the peak of her earning power, when she was pulling down $12,000 a week, Corinne wisely invested most of her money. Her knack for picking profitable properties caused "an old financier of Beverly Hills" to marvel in 1927, when she already owned $500,000 worth of real estate, "What a brain that girl has!"

A third marriage to Washington Redskins owner George P. Marshall in 1936 kept Corinne in the public eye. But she did not need the heir to a chain of laundries to stay center stage. A highly successful second career as an author with eleven published books and two best sellers did that for her.

In the 1950s, Corinne launched a personal crusade calling for the repeal of the Sixteenth Amendment. Throughout the ultraconservative Cold War decade, she was the best-known critic of the federal income tax.

But a day in court in 1966 stripped her of her credibility and caused many devoted admirers to question her sanity. Filing for divorce from her fourth husband, who happened to be twenty-six years her junior, she swore under oath that she was not Corinne Griffith but her much younger sister!

"Mary" claimed she had secretly taken her famous sibling's place in the mid-1920s after the sudden death of the movie star on location in Mexico. And Corinne Griffith stuck to that silly story until her dying day in 1979, when she passed away with $150 million in the bank.

19

# TED HEALY

## *Invented Three Stooges*

The name on the future comedian's birth certificate was either Ernest Lea Nash or Clarence Lee Nash; no one seems to know for sure. But there is no doubt that the birth certificate was issued in 1896 in the town of Kaufman, east of Dallas.

By the time little Ernest (or Clarence) was ready for school, the Nash family was living in Houston. He was twelve when they moved to New York City in 1908. Dazzled by the bright lights of Broadway, the teenager decided his future was in the exciting world of show business rather than on the nine-to-five treadmill of his coat-and-tie father.

Ernest/Clarence was a few months shy of his sixteenth birthday when he took the vaudeville plunge. Joined by pal Moses Horwitz, the future Moe Howard, he talked their way into male supporting roles in a water act called Annette Kellerman's Diving Girls.

The two friends soon found themselves out of work after one of the featured females broke her neck in a mistimed dive. The New Yorker and the Texan went their separate ways, but before long, the latter was back onstage as a comedian with a new name.

Ted Healy was a huge hit from the very outset. By the early 1920s, he was the highest-paid performer on the vaudeville circuit, earning a whopping $9,000 a week. (Keep in mind the inflation of the past century makes the 1920 dollar worth $100 today!) He was, however, no longer alone in the footlights, having added his new bride and a dog.

Healy reunited with Moe Howard in 1922, when he hired his old sidekick as a "stooge," an audience member who was secretly part of the act. Moe's brother Shemp was brought on board the next year as a heckler, followed in 1925 by Larry Fine, a violinist in real life.

Night after night, Healy and his "Three Stooges" had packed houses rolling in the aisles with the violent slapstick humor that had become their trademark. But by the end of the decade, Healy's drinking was out of control and the reason Shemp left the act.

Moe replaced his unhappy brother with another sibling whose stage alias was Curly. The Howards and Fine tolerated Healy's alcoholism and erratic behavior but could not stomach his stingy refusal to share the wealth. The trio permanently ended the one-sided relationship in 1934 upon learning their weekly hundred dollar stipend, which had to be split three ways, came out of the $30,000 Healy was pulling down.

There was animosity for awhile—Healy even sued his protégés for supposedly stealing his material—but mutual success softened the hard feelings. The Stooges were cracking up the country with their side-splitting films for Columbia, while Healy branched out into drama at MGM and had just signed a fat new contract with Warner Bros. in late 1936.

That same year, the screen actor married a woman almost half his age. Ever the impulsive type, Healy proposed to Betty Hickman within minutes of meeting the college coed, and the couple tied the knot in an Arizona ceremony after a midnight elopement.

According to Moe Howard, Healy had always wanted children. "He used to visit our homes and envied the fact that we were all married and had children," the Stooge wrote. "He loved kids and often gave Christmas parties for underprivileged youngsters and spent hundreds of dollars on toys."

The birth of his son John in December 1937 was a dream come true for the wannabe dad. When visiting hours were over five nights before Christmas, Healy kissed his wife and three-day-old baby goodnight and caught a cab for the Sunset Strip to spread the wonderful news and buy drinks all around.

By the time Healy arrived at the Trocadero, he was already as drunk as the proverbial skunk. What happened next depends upon who you believe.

In the official and widely accepted version, Healy got into a fight with three anonymous college boys in the parking lot of the Trocadero. He sustained serious injuries and despite the best efforts of his doctor and cardiologist died at home the next day.

In the unofficial but likely accurate version, Healy argued with actor Wallace Beery, Albert Broccoli (the producer who made his fortune with the

Bond movies) and a third man at the Trocadero bar. After Beery threw the first punch, Healy invited him outside to settle the matter.

But Broccoli, who had slipped out the door, was waiting and grabbed Healy in a bear hug. Beery proceeded to beat his helpless opponent to within an inch of his life before leaving him half conscious in a pool of his own blood.

Hollywood in those days was a company town, where the studios called the tune and everyone—cops, courts and newspapers included—danced to it. MGM was not about to let a box-office draw like Wallace Beery be tainted by scandal, much less stand trial.

The county coroner stuck to the script and ruled Ted Healy's death was caused by nothing more than a lifetime of heavy drinking. That verdict satisfied the police, and the investigation was closed, never to be reopened.

# 20
# BUDDY HOLLY AND WAYLON JENNINGS
## *Two Friends with Different Destinies*

A thousand people, mourners and the morbidly curious, squeezed into a Lubbock church on February 7, 1959, for the funeral of hometown rock and roller Buddy Holly.

A skinny musician from Littlefield would have given anything to have been there for his hero's send-off, but Waylon Jennings was stuck in the frozen North finishing the tour that had not missed a beat since the fatal plane crash four days earlier.

The two young Texans had known each other for going on five years after meeting in a Lubbock diner back in 1953, when Jennings was fifteen and Holly was a year older. Even though he was nearly the same age, Jennings looked up to the bespectacled singer/songwriter, and Holly reciprocated by looking after his younger admirer.

Holly's career took off like a rocket in 1957. "That'll Be the Day" shot to the top of the charts closely followed by "Peggy Sue," which crested at number three. Buddy and his band, the Crickets, performed both smash hits on *The Ed Sullivan Show* that December.

Just before Christmas 1958, Holly showed up at the Lubbock radio station where Jennings worked as a disc jockey. He handed him an electric bass guitar and announced, "You have two weeks to learn to play that thing."

That was Buddy's way of inviting Waylon to join him on the Winter Dance Party, a three-week tour of the upper Midwest due to start on January 23. It was a killer schedule, with twenty-five shows in twenty-five towns in twenty-five nights but a dream come true for the delighted deejay.

Lubbock, Texas, honored Buddy Holly with this bronze statue in the center of the West Texas Walk of Fame. *Library of Congress.*

Holly needed dependable musical backup after his recent falling out with the Crickets, and he knew he could count on Jennings, even if he had never touched a bass guitar. Tulsa guitarist Tommy Allsup and drummer "Goose" Bunch from Odessa filled the other two vacancies.

The three "new" Crickets arrived in New York by plane on January 15, 1959, for rehearsals. Allsup and Bunch shared a room in a Times Square hotel, while Jennings stayed with Holly and his wife of five months, Maria Elena.

In spite of the fact that Holly had been living in New York less than a year, Jennings was amazed at how fast he had adjusted to life in the Big Apple. Everything was alien to the lanky youth from West Texas, but nothing was stranger than the inhabitants.

Jennings found what he called in his 1996 autobiography "the New York attitude" hard to understand and even harder to take. After buying a pair of shoes from a sullen salesman, he asked, "Ain't you going to tell us to come back?"

Jennings never forgot the clerk's response. "Hillbilly, there's eight million people in this city, and if I never see you again it'll be too soon."

After a week in Manhattan, Jennings was ready to hit the road. The first stop for the Winter Dance Party was a ballroom in Milwaukee, where the dollar-a-ticket crowd saw their rock-and-roll favorites live and in person.

One-hit wonder Frankie Sardo opened the show followed by Beaumont disc jockey J.P. "Big Bopper" Richardson belting out his future classic "Chantilly Lace." Next came Dion and the Belmonts with their three Top Fifty songs and East Los Angeles teen Ritchie Valens with his huge hits "Donna" and "La Bamba." Then Buddy Holly and his brand-new band rocked the house for an hour.

Wisconsin, Minnesota and Iowa in the dead of winter were subzero iceboxes that took an awful toll on man and machine. On any given night, half of the stage talent and support staff were sick—"Goose" Bunch's feet actually froze!—and the tour bus gave up the ghost in the middle of nowhere.

Waylon Jennings was riding high in 1975 with two hit albums and a string of chart-busting singles. *RGD0006N03606, Houston Public Library, HMRC.*

By the time the road show reached Clear Lake, Iowa, on February 3, Holly had had it with all-night rides on the latest mass transit—a converted school bus with a broken heater. He chartered a private airplane to fly him and two passengers to Fargo, North Dakota.

Ritchie Valens won one seat on a coin flip with Tommy Allsup, and Holly assigned the other to his Texas Panhandle pal. But soft-hearted Jennings gave his spot on the warm plane to Richardson, who had come down with the flu.

"You're not going with me tonight, huh?" Holly joked at Jennings's expense. "Did you chicken out?" Jennings explained fear had nothing to do with it, that he was just doing the Big Bopper a favor.

"Well," Buddy said in good-natured jest, "I hope your damned bus freezes up again." Jennings answered in kind, "I hope your old plane crashes."

And that was just what it did less than ten minutes after takeoff, killing all on board.

"I just wanted to go home," Jennings remembered thirty-seven years later, "but they wouldn't stop the tour." The grief-stricken guitarist had to wait until he collected his pay after the final performance to return to Lubbock.

Waylon Jennings made the most of the forty-three years that act of kindness on a cold Iowa night bought him. At his death in 2002, he was a full-fledged legend in his own right with more than sixty albums and sixteen number one country music hits.

Buddy Holly would have been proud.

21

# JOHNNY HORTON

## *Eerie Premonition Came True*

John Gale Horton grew up on the move with a family of migrant farm workers, shuttling back and forth between the East Texas county of Cherokee, which they called home, and the produce fields of California, where he was born in 1925.

But the lettuce-picking gypsies did stay in one place long enough for their Johnny to finish high school at tiny Gallatin, just up the road from Rusk. Then he did something that most young people in his circumstances never dared to dream about—he went off to college.

According to Horton's biographers, who disagree on various details of his life, he attended Lon Morris Junior College in Jacksonville to study for the ministry, to play basketball or both. Although one claim that he received two dozen scholarship offers is probably an exaggeration, there can be no doubt that he was a talented athlete. Other stops on his campus tour were Baylor and Seattle University, and he may have been a member of both schools' basketball teams.

Deciding college was not for him, Horton wandered the West working odd jobs in California before winding up in Alaska in 1949. When he was not catching fish, a lifelong love, he was writing songs. Although he learned the guitar from his mother at age eleven, this was the first time that he took a serious interest in music.

Returning to his roots in 1950, Horton got up the nerve to enter a talent contest in Longview held by a radio deejay named Jim Reeves. First prize gave him the necessary confidence to try his luck as a guitar-plucking singer at small venues around East Texas.

The promising newcomer soon caught the eye of Fabor Robison, a manager and promoter with a mixed reputation. But Horton needed the guidance of someone with inside knowledge of the music world, and the smooth talker seemed to fill the bill.

After Robison landed a recording contract with Corman Records, Horton felt he had made the right choice. When the small label went out business before he cut a single record, he wondered whether it was bad luck or his manager's bad judgment.

To placate the unhappy performer, Robison formed his own company for the sole purpose of putting Horton's voice on vinyl. Then he convinced his client to reinvent himself as "The Singing Fisherman" and arranged appearances on radio and television in the Los Angeles area.

By 1952, Horton had come back from California and become a regular on the popular Shreveport-based radio program *The Louisiana Hayride*. In short order, his first wife left him, and Robison dumped him to take charge of Jim Reeves's blossoming career.

Horton filled the void with a new friend and mentor, the legendary Hank Williams, who rejoined *The Louisiana Hayride* after being kicked off the *Grand Ole Opry* for his drinking. After Williams's death in the backseat of a Cadillac on New Year's Eve 1952, his widow married his hero-worshipping protégé.

In spite of the exposure *The Louisiana Hayride* gave him, Horton's recording career was dead in the water. All that changed in 1955, when he signed with Tillman Franks. By the end of the year, he was under contract to Columbia Records and on his way to stardom with the classic "Honky Tonk Man."

Horton quickly proved he was no one-hit wonder. In less than a year, he followed "Honky Tonk Man" with "I'm a One-Woman Man," "I'm Coming Home" and "The Woman I Need," each climbing up the country music chart to numbers seven, eleven and nine, respectively.

Then the hits suddenly stopped coming. The drought did not break until the fall of 1958, when "All Grown Up" put Horton back in the Top Ten. But the best was yet to come.

With rock 'n roll squeezing out traditional country on the radio, Horton took a chance on storytelling songs. The risky move paid off big-time with "When It's Springtime in Alaska," which not only reached number one on the country chart but crossed over into the popular music ratings.

But it was "The Battle of New Orleans," which in 1959 sold a million copies in seven weeks, that cemented Horton's unique stature as the first country artist to bust the pop charts. "Johnny Reb" and "Sink the Bismarck" were also historical ballads and also dual Top Ten hits.

"North to Alaska" was released in early November 1960, but Horton would not be around to see it sell a million records too. In recent months, he had become obsessed with the haunting certainty that a drunk would end his life, and in the early hours of November 5, that bad dream came true on Highway 79 near the small town of Milano.

The car driven by Johnny Horton was hit head-on by a pickup truck with an intoxicated college student at the wheel. Horton and his two badly injured passengers were rushed to the hospital in nearby Cameron, but the singing sensation was dead on arrival. And, as too often seems to be the case, the drunk driver walked away with nothing worse than a few bumps and bruises.

22

# ROBERT E. HOWARD

## *Sword and Sorcery His Brainchild*

Bob Howard was born in 1906 at Peaster but left the "wide spot in the road" while still in diapers. His father, a footloose country doctor, dragged his frail wife and only child from town to town before finally settling down at Cross Plains, southeast of Abilene.

Physically weak and introverted as a child, Howard was what people back then called a "mama's boy." Mother and son developed, as one biographer put it, "a neurotic dependence on each other" that only grew stronger with time.

Howard was in his early teens in 1920 when oil was discovered inside the town limits of Cross Plains. Following the "boom" pattern repeated time and again across Texas, the quiet community of fifteen hundred mushroomed into a madhouse of ten thousand with the usual vice and violence.

Howard hated change on principle and yearned for the return of the familiar status quo, when the boom went bust and all the strange faces left town. Reflecting upon the unsettling experience, he wrote in 1931, "I'll say one thing about an oil boom. It will teach a kid that that life's a pretty rotten thing as quick as anything I can think of."

Rather than commute the thirty-three miles to Brownwood for his senior year of high school, Howard and his mother lived in a boardinghouse. After graduation in 1923, he spent two unsatisfying years in his hometown working a series of odd jobs.

Howard returned to Brownwood to study bookkeeping at Howard Payne College. Remembering his boyhood ambition to be a writer and a solemn vow never to "grind at some clock-punch job," he became a regular contributor to the student newspaper.

The turning point came in 1925 with the sale of his first story to *Weird Tales*. His reward for *Spear and Fang*, a tale of Cro-Magnons versus Neanderthals, was $18.

Encouraged by this initial success, Howard resolved to make his living as a full-time writer for the pulp magazine market. Neighbors complained that the incessant pounding of his typewriter, as well as his habit of shouting dialogue out loud, kept them awake at night, but the budding author paid them no mind. He was too busy bringing his fantasy world to life on paper.

The recluse, who never threw a punch, hated hunting and avoided contact with the opposite sex, spun exciting yarns about men of action that women always found irresistible. He began by writing about boxers, gunfighters and other real-life adventurers but soon progressed to pure fantasy, inventing his very own genre—sword and sorcery.

First came Solomon Kane, the Puritanical scourge of ghosts and vampires in Elizabethan England, who made his debut in 1928. Kane was followed the next year by King Kull, a warrior of fabled Atlantis who won the throne of Valusia before the continent sank beneath the waves. Bran Mak Morn, a savage barbarian who battled the Roman legions and supernatural enemies, appeared in 1932.

That was also the year Howard introduced his most popular character and the one for which he is best known today. He cast Conan the Cimmerian in the leading role of no fewer than seventeen action-packed epics during a prolific two-year period.

Howard did not put on pretentious airs when discussing his characters and, by implication, his writing. "They're simpler. You get them in a jam, and no one expects you to rack your brains inventing clever ways for them to extricate themselves. They are too stupid to do anything but cut, shoot or slug themselves into the clear."

He also insisted that his flights of fantasy were not the product of a vivid imagination but of his dreams. "I have lived in the Southwest all my life," he explained, "yet most of my dreams are laid in cold, giant lands of icy wastes and gloomy skies, and of wild, wind-swept fens and wildernesses over which sweep great sea-winds, and which are inhabited by shock-head savages with light fierce eyes."

Howard had the last laugh on the townspeople who made fun of him. At the depths of the Depression in 1935, he paid cash for a brand-new Chevrolet, an eye-popping purchase no one else in Cross Plains could afford.

A few months later, however, he was forced to face the fact that his mother was losing her long fight with tuberculosis. So despondent, he could not put a single word on paper and told a friend that he could not picture life without her. "Sometimes," he said, "it takes more courage to live than to die."

Howard went to see his mother on a June morning in 1936 and found she had lapsed into a coma. A tactless nurse informed him that she would never regain consciousness and had only hours to live.

Grief-stricken but clear-headed, Howard hurried home and typed his last words: "All fled, all done, So lift me on the pyre; The feast is over, The lamps expire."

He walked to his car, took a pistol from the glove compartment and shot himself in the head. Bob Howard died eight hours later in the bed next to his mother, and she joined him the next day. Mother and son were buried side by side in a Brownwood cemetery.

When Dr. Isaac Mordecai Howard passed away seven years later, he left a trunk containing his son's manuscripts to a fellow doctor. The royalties from Bob Howard's published works, which never amounted to more than $100 annually, went to him until his death in 1959.

By the early 1980s, the second doctor's elderly widow was getting six-figure checks in the mail every three months. Reprints of Robert E. Howard's fifty-year-old stories were selling like hotcakes thanks to a sword and sorcery revival and a couple of Conan movies starring a future governor of California.

23

# HOWARD HUGHES

## *Texas Tycoon in Movieland*

The virtually unknown chapter of the Houston billionaire's amazing life is his earliest. When Howard Hughes Sr. suddenly died of a heart attack in 1924, his son and sole heir inherited the company his father founded in 1905, the year young Howard was born. As soon as the courts declared him an "emancipated minor" and he took complete control of Hughes Tool, it was off to Hollywood to make a name for himself in motion pictures.

Putting his trust in an old family friend, the novice invested $40,000 in a movie that never sold a ticket. Actor Ralph Graves assured young Howard that *Swell Hogan*, a dull tale about a heart-of-gold derelict, would knock 'em in the aisles. But the bad script was even worse on celluloid, and Hughes hid the only print to keep the fiasco from ever being shown.

*Swell Hogan* did teach the would-be mogul that the film industry was no different than any other business. If he wanted the job done right, he had to do it himself.

Mastering every detail of production, Hughes soon completed his first feature entitled *Everybody's Acting*. The 1926 silent comedy netted enough to cover his *Swell Hogan* losses and gave his confidence a timely boost.

Hughes's next project was *Two Arabian Knights*, a comic adventure about a couple of American soldiers in the First World War. The costar was William Boyd, most remembered today as Hopalong Cassidy. *Two Arabian Knights* earned high marks from critics and audiences alike.

By the time his third and fourth flicks, *The Racket* and *The Mating Call*, reached the screen in 1928, Hughes was already hard at work on the aviation epic *Hell's Angels*. Vowing not to let costs stand in the way of making a true-to-life flight film, he spared no expense in assembling the largest private air force in the world for the breathtaking combat scenes.

Hughes not only called the shots as director, but also insisted on demonstrating the desired aerial acrobatics. His crack-up during a particularly tricky maneuver nearly caused collective heart failure on the set. Before he walked away from the crash, a crew member recalled quipping, "I thought for a moment that we had all lost our meal ticket."

Three stunt pilots were not as fortunate. One burned to death when he struck power lines, another ran out of gas in mid-air and a third perished in a simulated crash dive that turned into the real thing.

*Hell's Angels* established Hughes as a first-rate producer/director and transformed an unknown platinum blonde named Jean Harlow into a 1930s superstar. Starting out as a silent movie, two and a half years and $4 million later it broke the sound barrier for the Texan with the deep pockets.

Hughes hurriedly cranked out several more box-office hits, though none matched *Hell's Angels*, which he always considered his masterpiece. At the peak of his cinematic career, the unpredictable tycoon suddenly gave up moviemaking for his new obsession—flying.

In 1939, Hughes decided to mount a movie comeback with a Western loosely based on the life of Billy the Kid. Remembering the gold mine he had discovered in Harlow, he gambled on casting complete unknowns for the parts of Billy and his girlfriend Rio.

Gummo, the Marx brother who never appeared in his siblings' comedies, introduced Hughes to Jack Buetel, a twenty-three-year-old nobody from Dallas, and Hughes signed the fellow Texan on the spot.

Hughes personally picked the female lead from a pile of publicity pictures. At nineteen, Earnestine Jane Geraldine Russell did not have so much as a second of acting experience, but Hughes could have cared less about her thespian credentials.

Jane Russell soon learned why she won the intense competition for the coveted role. When she complained the promotional photographs always stressed her thirty-eight-inch bustline, Hughes explained, "That's the way to sell a picture."

The Hays Office, official guardian of movie morality, went over the script with a fine-tooth comb. The watchdogs advised Hughes to tone down the dialogue and warned "care must be taken to avoid sexual suggestiveness."

A private viewing of *The Outlaw* in early 1941 sent the skittish censors through the roof. The chief inspector complained in a letter to Hughes: "I

Howard Hughes had it all—youth, money, looks and his sanity—when this photograph was taken in 1939. *RG1005, Houston Public Library, HMRC.*

have never seen anything quite so unacceptable as the shots of the breasts of the character Rio. Throughout almost half the picture the girl's breasts, which are large and prominent, are shockingly uncovered."

The most objectionable frames ended up on the cutting room floor, and *The Outlaw* received the mandatory "Seal of Approval." Then, to spite the censors, Hughes plastered a larger-than-life image of his buxom leading lady on thousands of billboards with the caption, "How'd you like to tussle with Russell?"

After two years of hype and hysteria, *The Outlaw* was finally released. It turned out to be just another Western and not a very good one at that.

24

# CAROLYN JONES

## *Television's Morticia*

*The Addams Family*, an offbeat television comedy about the ghouls next door, premiered on September 20, 1964, with a motion picture actress from the Texas Panhandle in the role of Morticia.

Carolyn Sue Jones was born into an unhappy Amarillo home in April 1930. Four years later, the head of the house walked out, forcing his abandoned wife and two little girls to move in with her parents.

Jones inherited an almost fanatical fascination with the movies from her mother, who named her daughters after film stars Carol Lombard and Bette Davis. Asthma attacks, which kept her in bed for weeks at a time, often caused the girl to miss first-run features in the downtown theaters, but she made up for that by reading every fan magazine she could get her hands on.

Carolyn Jones decided early in life that she wanted to be a movie actress and pursued her dream with precocious purpose. She consistently stole the show in high school plays and won numerous awards in speech, poetry and dramatic reading.

Following graduation from Amarillo High in 1947, Jones was accepted by the Pasadena Playhouse, the prestigious pipeline to the moviemaking machine. With the enthusiastic encouragement of her relatives, she spent the next three years learning her chosen craft and gaining practical experience with summer stock companies.

Jones did not have to wait long to be "discovered." Spotted by a talent scout in a local theater production, she passed her screen test and signed a six-month contract with Paramount Studios. Her big-screen debut in the

Carolyn Jones was a natural blond when she arrived in Hollywood in 1952. *RGD5F6692, Houston Public Library, HMRC.*

1952 flick *The Turning Point* was a cause for celebration in Amarillo, where, according to her sister, their grandparents "danced around the living room" and their mother "cried."

But Jones wound up out of work and broke when Paramount did not renew her contract. For the next couple of years, she succeeded in paying the rent while sharpening her skills on some of television's top shows, such as *The Millionaire*, *The Colgate Comedy Hour*, *Mr. and Mrs. North* and *Lux Video Theatre*.

The year 1953 was a red-letter one for Jones. She turned a small part in the 3-D horror movie *House of Wax* into a career boost and married a struggling screenwriter from Dallas named Aaron Spelling.

A Columbia Pictures executive felt Jones was perfect for a major part in *From Here to Eternity*. But the night before her audition, the Texan was hospitalized with pneumonia, and the Oscar-winning role went to Donna Reed.

Disappointed but not discouraged, Jones kept plugging away, and her hard work was rewarded with bigger parts in better pictures. She appeared in *Desiree* with Marlon Brando, *The Seven Year Itch* with Marilyn Monroe and the science fiction classic *Invasion of the Body Snatchers* before cutting her blond hair short and dyeing it black for *The Bachelor Party*. Though on screen for a mere eight minutes, her riveting performance in the 1957 drama earned an Academy Award nomination for Best Supporting Actress.

Jones did not take home the Oscar but as a consolation prize found herself suddenly in demand. She was Mickey Rooney's gun moll in *Baby-Face Nelson*, Natalie Wood's best friend in *Marjorie Morningstar*, the object of Frank Sinatra's affection in *A Hole in the Head* and Elvis Presley's romantic interest in his best movie, *King Creole*.

She was one of Hollywood's busiest and best-paid character actresses, but she chose to risk it all for the chance to be a leading lady. She gambled on a box-office flop ironically entitled *Career*, and the mistake cost her dearly.

Husband Aaron's career finally took off just as Carolyn's stalled. They separated in the fall of 1963 and divorced the following summer. She could have taken the future king of prime-time television to the cleaners but chose not to ask for alimony.

At this low point in Carolyn's life came the invitation to join the cast of *The Addams Family*, which hit the airwaves the same month as *The Munsters* and *Bewitched*. John Astin, her costar and a big fan, put his finger on the actress's deadpan appeal: "What made Carolyn so perfect in the role of Morticia was that wicked sense of humor she had."

Makeup aged Carolyn Jones decades for the 1959 television program *The David Niven Show*. She stood in front of a painting showing how she really looked at the time. *RGD5F6692, Houston Public Library, HMRC.*

*The Addams Family* was still riding high in the ratings when ABC inexplicably canceled the series at the end of the second season. Alone and in limbo, Jones married her vocal coach and retired to Palm Springs.

Seven years later, she returned to Hollywood to try a comeback at age forty-six. She found plenty of work on the small screen with guest appearances and made-for-television movies. She had just settled into a continuing role on a daytime soap opera when she was diagnosed with colon cancer.

For two years, Carolyn Jones battled the dreadful disease with courage, determination and a smile. But she ultimately lost the fight for her life and died at home in 1983 at the age of fifty-three.

25

# SPANKY McFARLAND

## Texas's Own "Little Rascal"

A small but prominent notice on the front page of the April 11, 1933 edition of a Dallas daily let the whole town know five-year-old Tommy Bond was throwing a party for fellow *Our Gang* cast member Spanky McFarland, age three.

The idea for a comedy series based on kids just being themselves came to Hal Roach one afternoon in 1921. The silent movie pioneer was staring out the window of his Culver City, California office, when it suddenly dawned on him that a group of children at play had mesmerized him for a good fifteen minutes.

No one in the short history of the motion picture industry had ever simply turned youngsters loose in front of the camera. That was, in essence, what Roach's senior director did in bringing his boss's radical concept to life on the silver screen.

As a rule, Robert F. McGowan did not show the script to the pint-sized actors, especially those who had not yet learned to read. Instead, he patiently explained the next scene seconds before calling "action" and directed the tiny thespians with a megaphone.

The end result was not the standard film fare of children pretending to be adults but kids in their "natural state" with grown-ups out of the picture. Audiences loved the captivating two-reel (twenty-minute) "shorts" right from the start, and reviewers beat the drum for "lots more of those *Our Gang* comedies."

*Hal Roach's Rascals* was actually the original title, but the public as well as the news media insisted upon *Our Gang*. That is why for the first ten years the comedy series had two official names, until the creator finally scuttled his preference in 1932.

In the beginning, the cast was one of convenience, consisting of the sons and daughters of studio employees and their friends' offspring. The sole exception was Ernie "Sunshine Sammy" Morrison, the first black actor of any age awarded a long-term contract, who soon gave way to Allen "Farina" Hoskins, the most popular *Our Gang* player of the 1920s.

Hal Roach had the foresight and judgment to embrace change rather than resist it. He knew, for example, that moviegoers would love hearing the sound of their favorite *Our Gang* characters' voices. The box-office receipts for the first "all-talking" episode in April 1929 proved him right and more than paid for the expensive new technology.

Roach also understood that child actors did not stay small and endearing indefinitely and that adolescence made most of them something other than adorable. He solved this unavoidable problem with a nonstop, nationwide search for fresh faces.

George McFarland was already an accomplished model at the tender age of three and a familiar face on billboards around Dallas as the poster child for Wonder Bread. Replying to a magazine advertisement request for photographs of "cute kids," McFarland's aunt mailed professional pictures of her nephew to the Hal Roach Studios in January 1931.

In short order, the Texas toddler was invited to California, given a screen test, which he aced, and put under contract. "Sonny," as he was known back home, became Spanky and a scene-stealing addition to the *Our Gang* lineup.

At about the same time, a second Texan was discovered coming out of a Dallas movie theater with his mother. Tommy Bond was five, going on six, when a talent scout informed his surprised parent, "He's got a great face. You ought to take him to Hollywood to meet Hal Roach."

Thanks to his grandmother, who drove him all the way to the West Coast over dirt roads and through flash floods, Bond did meet Roach in person. He was signed on the spot and initially cast as mild-mannered Tommy. Later, after a two-year hiatus during which he returned to Dallas and public school, Bond returned as the memorable bully Butch.

The third Texan to join *Our Gang* was Eugene Gordon Lee, of Fort Worth. In 1935, the adopted son of an embalmer and a stenographer won the part of Spanky's little brother due to his strong resemblance at eighteen months to the star of the series.

Spanky McFarland had two years left as the favorite *Our Gang* cast member when this photograph was snapped in 1936. *RGD5F3940, Houston Public Library, HMRC.*

Renamed Porky, he appeared in forty-two comedies before a growth spurt turned him into a has-been at five. Even though McFarland was twice his age, the "baby brother" could now look him straight in the eye. His movie career over before he entered first grade, Lee was replaced by Mickey Gubitosi, better known today as Robert Blake.

McFarland's small stature and undeniable talent made it possible for him to play Spanky until the comparatively ripe old age of fourteen. When he at last departed in 1942, *Our Gang*, sold by Hal Roach to MGM in 1938, had only two years remaining in its remarkable run.

But television brought the timeless comedy back for a well-deserved encore in the 1950s. A new generation of fans, the so-called baby boomers, laughed until it hurt at the antics of *The Little Rascals*.

Of the three Texas-born performers, Spanky McFarland benefitted the most from the *Our Gang* revival before a fatal heart attack in 1993. Tommy Bond, who spent four decades behind the camera in television production, and Gordon Lee, who dropped out of sight until the 1980s, were lifelong friends who died a month apart in 2005.

26

# ANN MILLER

## *Tap Dancing Marvel*

In a September 1939 review of George White's *Scandals of 1939*, a Broadway critic reserved his highest praise for a teenager from Texas named Ann Miller, who stopped the show every night with her high-energy tap dance.

The future fixture of Hollywood musicals in the 1930s and 1940s was born Lucille Ann Collier at her grandparents' place near Nacogdoches. The year was 1923, and that was important because she would later change it in order to find work in Tinsel Town.

Her disappointed dad, who had his heart set on a son, insisted upon calling her Johnnie, and the rest of the family went along to keep the peace. She was just three years old when her mother Clara bought her dance lessons to strengthen the child's tiny legs, which had been weakened by rickets.

Little Johnnie Collier loved to dance and loved it even more after a chance meeting at a local theater with Bill "Bojangles" Robinson. The legendary vaudevillian, who is credited with creating the tap dance, gave the girl a quick demonstration and a few choice words of encouragement, but that was enough to change her life.

Johnnie was ten when she came home from visiting her grandmother to find her cheating father in the arms of another woman. The moment her hearing-impaired mother walked in the door, the girl shouted at the top of her lungs, "Mother, pack your bags!"

Ann Miller in a still shot from the 1953 musical *Kiss Me Kate. RGD5F3647, Houston Public Library, HMRC.*

Mother and daughter left the next morning and never looked back. They drove to Hollywood, sold the car for living expenses and began beating the bushes for gainful employment.

Job prospects were bleak for a deaf single mother in the middle of the Depression. Johnnie, on the other hand, had reached her adult height of five foot seven and possessed a maturity far beyond her eleven years. She had no trouble finding work as a dancer in a club that fronted for an upstairs gambling den.

Times were tough, but the runaways survived on Johnnie's weekly wage of $25 and the motherlode of tips from customers blown away by her tap dancing. Before walk-on appearances in two motion pictures, Johnnie adopted the stage persona of "Ann Miller," and that was the name she danced under in the 1936 film *Devil on Horseback*.

With her brunette beauty and dazzling talent, it was only a matter of time until Miller was "discovered." She had yet to turn fourteen when actress Lucille Ball and comedian Benny Rubin "found" her dancing at a popular San Francisco nightclub.

The redhead later adored by the television viewing audience as Lucy introduced her underage protégée to all the right people at RKO Studios. With a fake birth certificate provided by her lawyer father in Texas that "proved" she was eighteen, Miller soon had a seven-year contract and a part in *New Faces of 1937*.

That busy year and the next, Ann Miller danced with Ginger Rogers in *Stage Door* and rubbed shoulders on the set with the entire stable of RKO stars, including Katherine Hepburn, Jimmy Stewart, Jean Arthur and even the Marx Brothers. But budget-conscious RKO decided she was not worth $200 a week and cut her loose.

Miller was free to try something she had been dreaming about—Broadway. An absolute sensation in *Scandals of 1939*, she was the first person George Abbott thought of when RKO hired him to direct *Too Many Girls*. Stingy studio bosses that balked at a measly $200 a week now had to pay her $3,000 fifty-two times a year.

Miller spent the war years at Republic, where she gave Gene Autry his first on-screen kiss, and Columbia, where she made patriotic puff pieces intended to boost home-front morale. Harry Cohn, the studio head at Columbia, wanted to showcase her in an expensive full-color extravaganza, but she turned him down to marry an heir to a steel fortune.

She was eight months pregnant the night her husband, in a drunken rage, threw her down a flight of stairs, breaking her back. She gave birth in a steel harness, but the baby lived only a few hours. Her husband's wealthy relatives stole the tiny body, and for the next half century, the grieving mother had no idea where her child was buried.

Miller filed for divorce from her hospital bed, and upon her release, she went to work for MGM. She actually danced in a back brace in *Easter Parade*, the

1948 box-office smash costarring Fred Astaire and Judy Garland. Rewarded with a seven-year contract, she turned in memorable performances in such musicals as *On the Town* (1949), *Small Town Girl* (1952), *Hit the Deck* (1955) and *The Opposite Sex* (1956).

After her movie career wound down, Miller traveled the world as MGM's "Goodwill Ambassador." Under "occupation," her passport listed "star," which must have raised a lot of eyebrows going through customs.

In 1979, at the (real) age of fifty-six, Miller made an epic comeback in *Sugar Babies*. The wildly popular musical costarring Mickey Rooney ran for two years on Broadway and seven more on the road.

Not long before she died from lung cancer in 2004, Ann Miller joked, "I can still tap, but who wants to pay an old lady to tap sitting down?" Five years earlier, a friend had found her missing baby's grave, and in death, mother and child were reunited at last.

27

# ROGER MILLER

## "King of the Road"

The Depression-era baby was still in diapers when his father died in his twenties from spinal meningitis. Miller's destitute mother passed out her three sons like door prizes, one each to a trio of brothers-in-law, and disappeared from her children's lives.

That was why Roger Dean Miller grew up on a farm in western Oklahoma instead of his birthplace, Fort Worth. He never felt at home with his adoptive family, who treated him like an extra pair of cotton picking hands.

The lonely youngster's only friend was Sheb Wooley, a local lad fifteen years his senior and a cousin by marriage. Wooley, whose claim to fame was the novelty hit "Purple People Eater," taught the boy how to play the guitar and bought him his first fiddle.

Miller ran away from the unhappy home the summer before his senior year of high school. Before long, he was behind bars, arrested for stealing a guitar. Given the choice of jail or the Army, he picked military service.

The day he was discharged, Miller caught a bus for the capital of country music. The ex-soldier found a job as a bellhop in a Nashville hotel. Anyone trapped in the elevator with him instantly became a captive audience for his latest lyrics.

Miller eventually got his foot in the door as a fiddler for Minnie Pearl's road band. Soon after that, he met George Jones at a radio station, and the established star graciously listened to several of his creations. The fellow Texan liked what he heard and arranged an audition for Miller with Mercury-Starday Records.

Roger Miller was on top of the world when he sat down for an interview with the *Houston Post* in 1968. *RGD0006N00024A, Houston Public Library, HMRC.*

The music executives were impressed enough to schedule a recording session in Houston. On the car ride to Texas, Jones and Miller collaborated on a number of songs, including "Tall, Tall Trees," which Jones cut in the spring of 1957.

Married and with a baby on the way, Miller reluctantly decided to put his dream on hold. But even in Amarillo, where he worked as a fireman, destiny tracked him down. In less than a year, Ray Price hired him as a tour singer with the Cherokee Cowboys.

Back in Nashville, Miller wrote "Invitation to the Blues" for Price, which shot up to number three on the country music chart. In short order, he turned out Top Ten hits for Ernest Tubb, Faron Young and Jim Reeves.

But as the 1950s drew to a close, the successful songwriter was far from satisfied. He wanted to perform his own material, and RCA agreed to help him to do exactly that.

However, except for "When Two Worlds Collide," number six in 1961, the Top Ten was beyond Miller's reach. RCA dropped him in late 1963, about the same time as his marriage hit the rocks.

Miller took the setback in stride because he already had taken a different career path—television. A guest appearance on *The Tonight Show*, courtesy of substitute host Jimmy Dean, had left millions of viewers in stitches. America, it seemed, could not get enough of his offbeat sense of humor.

To pursue his dream and move to California, Miller needed cash in a hurry, and a pop music subsidiary of Mercury Records solved his problem. Smash Records offered him $100 a song for fifteen cuts to be recorded in two back-to-back sessions.

That historic songfest on January 10–11, 1964, produced "Dang Me," written in four minutes in an Arizona hotel room, and "Chug-a-Lug." Within six months, the first conquered both the pop and country charts, and the second repeated the impressive feat that fall.

On November 3, 1964, Miller recorded his signature classic. "King of the Road" was released in early 1965 and took the music world by storm, staying atop the country chart for five weeks and peaking at number four on the pop list. By May, it had sold a million copies.

The previous month, Miller won five Grammys, the Oscar of the music industry. He proved he was no flash in the pan by adding six more in 1965 for a career total of eleven.

In September 1966, Miller's postponed wish was granted with a variety show of his own on network television. But he could not get the hang of the small-screen format, and NBC canceled *The Roger Miller Show* after thirteen weeks.

A fresh challenge brought Miller out of semiretirement in the early 1980s. A college professor talked him into writing the score for a musical based on the Mark Twain character Huckleberry Finn.

*Big River* was, according a bowled-over critic, Miller's "crowning achievement." The Tony he received for Best Score was the first ever awarded to a country music artist.

While on a comeback tour in 1991, Miller was diagnosed with lung cancer. He put up a good-natured fight but succumbed to the disease the following October.

Before his premature death at the age of fifty-six, Roger Miller said he did not care how he was remembered. "I just don't want to be forgotten," he said. With so many devoted fans, there is no danger of that ever happening.

28

# AUDIE MURPHY

## "Fugitive from the Law of Averages"

For a teenaged autograph seeker, he once scribbled, "Audie L. Murphy—a fugitive from the law of averages." Twenty-five years later, fate caught up with the sharecropper's son whose battlefield exploits won a chestful of medals and worldwide fame.

The birth of their seventh child in 1924 was a mixed blessing at best for the dirt-poor Murphys of rural Hunt County. An undependable provider, Pat Murphy was easily distracted from his domestic duties and just like clockwork would vanish for weeks at a time.

Shelter was a clapboard house with paper-thin walls and later a crudely remodeled boxcar. During the Depression, the Murphys survived on the charity of area churches.

Audie Murphy did not see the inside of a classroom until he was nine years old, but even so, his small stature shielded him from the taunts of the younger kids. His formal education was interrupted in the fifth grade, when the youngster was forced to contribute a paycheck. Once again his father had disappeared, but this time for good.

Murphy's mother died at forty-nine in the spring of 1941, an early grave her reward for a harsh hand-to-mouth existence. The three younger children were packed off to an orphanage, leaving grief-stricken Murphy on his own.

The eager enlistee was turned down the following year by the Marines and Army paratroopers. With his baby face and pint-size stature—five feet five inches and a hundred and ten pounds— Murphy looked closer to thirteen than his actual seventeen years. But another birthday satisfied the

The most decorated U.S. soldier of World War II looked happy to be home in the summer of 1945. *RGD5F220, Houston Public Library, HMRC.*

local Army recruiter, and in June 1942, the excited volunteer boarded the bus for basic training.

After a brief taste of action in North Africa, the infantryman took part in the Allied invasion of Sicily and the Italian mainland in mid-1943. During the next year and a half, the diminutive dogface wrote an amazing new chapter in the annals of American heroism.

While U.S. forces methodically purged Italy of Germans, Murphy exhibited extraordinary courage and daring. His single-handed destruction of an enemy tank in March 1944 merited the Bronze Star, the first of a record collection of combat citations.

A remarkable marksman, Murphy won countless sniper duels. Teaming up with a buddy fluent in German, he slipped behind enemy lines in the dead of night to snare enemy soldiers for interrogation.

But the Texan's dramatic destiny lay in the blood-drenched meadows of southern France. Five months of constant fighting earned him the Distinguished Service Cross, a pair of Silver Stars and a chestful of lesser medals as well as two wounds. These deeds, however, only served as a dress rehearsal for an unforgettable solo performance on January 26, 1945.

That morning, Murphy, who had risen in rank from private to first lieutenant, assumed command of his original company. Hours later, the unit faced annihilation from a column of German armor. Ordering his men into a nearby forest, Lieutenant Murphy remained at his hazardous post and relayed coordinates over a field telephone to a distant artillery battery.

When the barrage failed to halt the German advance, Murphy grabbed a machine gun atop a burning tank destroyer. Firing nonstop for an hour, he repulsed wave after wave of attackers. Sustaining at least fifty casualties from the one-man army, the incredulous Germans beat a hasty retreat, leaving Murphy without so much as a scratch.

Audie Murphy after transformation from war hero to motion picture actor specializing in shoot-'em-ups. *RGD5F220, Houston Public Library, HMRC.*

Eleven days after receiving the Congressional Medal of Honor and the French Legion of Merit, an awe-struck Audie was greeted in San Antonio by a quarter of a million cheering Texans. The shy twenty-one-year-old with the juvenile good looks was suddenly a national hero, the most decorated soldier in American history.

A surprise invitation from actor James Cagney offered him a welcome break from the hectic schedule of parades and banquets. The stay at the film legend's California estate concluded with the guest choosing Hollywood over a military career or veterinary studies.

Critics in general applauded Murphy for stand-out performances in *The Red Badge of Courage* and *To Hell and Back*, the film version of his best-selling autobiography, which set a box-office record for Universal Studios that stood for the next twenty years until surpassed by the blockbuster *Jaws*.

Low-budget Westerns soon became his bread and butter. Between 1949 and 1967, the hardworking actor appeared in forty-four motion pictures, all but a dozen sagebrush sagas. He tried his luck on television in 1961, but his series *Whispering Smith* lasted just one season.

For Murphy, the rosy life of a movie star concealed a bushel of thorns. Painful souvenirs of his European experience were insomnia and chronic stomach problems. A fourth-grade education ill prepared him for business, and he declared bankruptcy in 1968.

On May 28, 1971, a twin-engine private plane carrying the actor and five others plowed into a fog-shrouded Virginia mountain, killing all on board. In a melancholy coincidence, confirmation of Audie Murphy's tragic death came on Memorial Day.

# 29
# ROY ORBISON

## *"The Voice of God"*

The year was 1936, and the place was Vernon, just this side of the Red River. Orbie Lee and Nadine Orbison welcomed the newest addition to their working-class family, a boy they named Roy Kelton.

The defense plants drew the breadwinner to Fort Worth during World War II, but he pulled up stakes again after butter became more important than guns. The Orbisons moved out west to Wink, a tiny oil-patch community not far from where the New Mexico and Texas state lines come to a point.

Music was as much a part of Roy Orbison's childhood as corn bread and molasses. He learned to play the guitar from his father at six and seven years later formed his first band, the Wink Westerners. It was not long before the teenaged musicians were out of the garage and on the radio in nearby Kermit.

Orbison received his diploma from Wink High School in 1954 and attended North Texas State for a couple of semesters. But Denton was too far from home, and he transferred the next year to a junior college in Odessa.

The revived Westerners caught fire with weekly half-hour shows on two television stations. A guest performer, twenty-three-year-old Johnny Cash, liked what he heard and referred the group to his producer, Sam Phillips, of Sun Records.

At first, the rockabilly pioneer wanted nothing to do with Orbison and his playmates but changed his mind after listening to "Ooby Dooby," a catchy tune the Wink wonders recorded in a New Mexico studio. The star maker invited the Westerners to Memphis, where he signed them up and changed their name to the Teen Kings.

Orbison pictured himself following in the footsteps of Phillips protégés like Elvis Presley, Carl Perkins, Jerry Lee Lewis and his benefactor Cash. But after making a modest splash with the rerelease of "Ooby Dooby," the Teen Kings fell out of favor.

His friends returned to West Texas, but Orbison stayed in Memphis and joined the ranks of the music capital's struggling songwriters. He wrote "Claudette," named after his new wife, for the Everly Brothers, who put it on the flip side of their huge hit "All I Have to Do Is Dream."

In 1957, Orbison teamed up with Midland native Joe Melson, and the talented Texans invented a new musical genre—the rock ballad. The prolific pair penned a passel of Top Twenty songs for a small-time label, Monument Records.

Owner Fred Foster rewarded Orbison with a second shot as a singer, and he responded in March 1960 with the unforgettable "Only the Lonely." The haunting ballad soared to number two in the United States and to the top of the charts in Great Britain, where rock 'n' roll was all the rage.

Roy Orbison memorialized in outdoor mural in hometown of Wink, Texas. *Library of Congress.*

Roy Orbison, at twenty-four, was on his way to international stardom. In three head-spinning years, he sold millions of 45s with smash hits such as "Blue Angel," "Running Scared," "Crying" and "Blue Bayou"—all Orbison-Melson collaborations.

Overcoming his fear of live performances, the shy vocalist with the amazing four-octave range played sold-out concerts at home and abroad. He toured Europe in 1963 with an unknown British quartet, and it was Orbison who encouraged the Beatles to come to the former colonies.

One of the few American recording artists to survive the subsequent "British Invasion," "The Big O" actually thrived. "Oh, Pretty Woman," number one in 1964, set a record for the most copies sold in the first ten days and ultimately totaled seven million in sales.

Orbison's unusually pale complexion and ever-present sunglasses spawned rumors that persist to this day. He was neither, as some believed, an albino nor was he blind.

Times change, and so do tastes in music, as Orbison found out in the late 1960s. However, for every American fan he lost, there were at least two foreigners to take his place. From the Netherlands, site of the biggest Roy Orbison fan club on the planet, to Australia, where he was a permanent fixture on the charts, he retained a large and loyal worldwide following.

The slump in his U.S. popularity coincided with terrible tragedies only two years apart. Claudette Orbison was killed in a motorcycle accident in the summer of 1966, and two of their three sons burned to death in a fire at the family residence in September 1968.

Grief kept Orbison out of the limelight and the studio for a long time. He remarried, had two more boys by his second wife and gradually picked up the pieces of his shattered personal life.

Open-heart surgery in 1978 bought the ailing performer ten more years. He lived long enough to experience a gratifying resurgence in popularity and the appreciation of his peers. In the late 1980s, he was invited to join the Traveling Wilburys, a supergroup featuring George Harrison, Tom Petty, Bob Dylan and Jeff Lynne, of Electric Light Orchestra. The band's debut album was released on October 18, 1988, preceding Orbison's fatal heart attack by less than two months.

"His voice could jar a corpse, always leave you muttering to yourself something like, 'Man! I don't believe it!'" marveled Bob Dylan. Elvis Presley once called him "the greatest singer in the world," but to Barry Gibb of the Bee Gees, Roy Orbison was simply "the voice of God."

30

# BUCK OWENS

## *Borrowed the Donkey's Name*

On a farm near Sherman, just a short distance from the Red River, Alvis Edgar Owens Jr. was born in 1929. As a small boy, he announced that he preferred the name of the family donkey to his own. His parents went along, and after that, everyone called him "Buck."

Driven west by the Great Depression and the Dust Bowl, the Owens clan headed for California in 1937 but got only as far as Mesa, Arizona. That was where Buck Owens quit school in the ninth grade to work on the family farm and to master the guitar, his real interest.

By his late teens, Owens's picking had improved to the point that he was playing once a week on a radio show and most nights in the honky-tonks around Phoenix. At nineteen, he married a country music singer, the first of his four wives, and by 1950 had fathered two sons.

To support his growing family, Owens drove trucks through the San Joaquin Valley in Central California. He liked the looks of Bakersfield so much that he talked his wife into moving there in 1951.

The club scene in his adopted hometown provided Owens with plenty of paying gigs and the opportunity to form his first band, the Schoolhouse Playboys. Bakersfield's close proximity to Hollywood made regular round-trips to Capitol Records possible, enabling Buck to sit in on recording sessions with artists like Tennessee Ernie Ford, Faron Young, Wanda Jackson, Gene Vincent and Sonny James, to mention a few.

But Owens was not satisfied with being a studio musician and a big fish in the small Bakersfield pond. He jumped at the chance to sign with

Capitol Records but was bitterly disappointed by the lack of success his initial singles enjoyed.

Convinced his recording career was over before it had even begun, Owens relocated to Tacoma, Washington, with his second wife in 1958. During the day, he spun records and sold advertising for a radio station and at night performed in any club that let him onstage.

Late that year, Capitol Records decided to give Owens another shot, and this time allowed him to use the steel guitar and fiddle so essential to his honky-tonk sound. To everyone's surprise, a single from that second-chance session titled "Second Fiddle" caught fire and climbed to number twenty-four on the *Billboard* country chart.

Owens soon proved he was no flash in the pan with "Under Your Spell Again," which peaked at number four. That was right about the time he moved back to Bakersfield, followed by Don Rich, a Tacoma-based guitarist and vocalist who became his closest collaborator and best friend.

On the strength of several more Top Ten hits and brisk sales of his first album, Owens and his new buddy went on the road. After months of making do with "house" musicians, the duo patiently pieced together a band of their own that a bass player by the name of Merle Haggard called the Buckaroos.

Owens knew it would take a number one single to put him on top, but he did not think "Act Naturally" was the song that would do it. Don Rich managed to change his mind, and the result was the first of an incredible streak of fifteen consecutive number one hits that spanned four chart-busting years.

Halfway through the 1960s, Buck Owens and the Buckaroos were the hottest act in popular music. They sold records and albums by the truckload and performed live in front of packed houses of every description—small clubs to giant arenas—nearly every night of the year.

In 1969, two Canadian television producers dreamed up a cornball country music version of Rowan and Martin's *Laugh-In* as a summer substitute for the Smothers Brothers. Owens argued that he did not have time for the show with his hectic schedule, a problem the producers solved by having him tape his segments twice a year.

*Hee Haw* turned out to be the Smothers Brothers' permanent replacement, with ratings that went through the roof. After a two-year run on CBS, it was cancelled in the network's purge of programs with a rural theme. But *Hee Haw* found new life in syndication and stayed on the air until 1992.

Since the tragic death of Don Rich in a motorcycle accident in 1974, Owens had only been going through the motions. Other than *Hee Haw*,

Buck Owens (left) and *Hee Haw* cohost Roy Clark. *DeGolyer Library, Southern Methodist University.*

on which he continued to appear until 1986, his career had come to a screeching halt.

Owens finally broke his silence on the subject of Rich's premature passing in the late 1990s: "He was like a brother, a son and a best friend. I think my music life ended when he did."

In 2006, hours after what turned out to be a farewell performance at his Crystal Palace restaurant, club and museum in Bakersfield, Buck Owens died in his sleep of an apparent heart attack. The Dust Bowl refugee was seventy-six years old.

The stretch of highway that runs through his birthplace of Sherman has been renamed Buck Owens Freeway in his memory.

31

# GEORGE SESSIONS PERRY

## *Could Not Outswim His Demons*

The future novelist and magazine contributor was born and raised in the Central Texas town of Rockdale. His father, owner of two drugstores, and artistic mother doted on their only child, gladly granting his every wish.

Even though the Perrys did not live directly off the land, the sensitive boy empathized with the sharecroppers and tenant farmers of Milam County. Two of his early unpublished novels are scathing indictments of the rural poverty witnessed in his youth.

The head of the Perry household died of Bright's disease, which destroys the kidneys, in 1921 when George was eleven years old. His emotionally fragile mother soon married again but took her own life in 1923.

According to a childhood friend, George Perry felt personally responsible for the tragic death of his beloved mother: "First, because his failure to give her the affection she needed caused her to remarry, and then because he did not kill the husband who had made her so unhappy."

The orphan rebelled against his domineering and ill-tempered grandmother and the uncle who rationed the income from his inheritance. In response to Perry's bad behavior and poor grades, the surrogate father packed him off to Allen Academy in Bryan, where he shaped up and finished high school.

After attending Southwestern University, Purdue and the University of Houston, Perry quit college altogether and spent six months selling shoes and lampshades in Chicago. Deciding to see the world, he worked his way across the Atlantic aboard a freighter but was caught without a passport in France and deported to the United States.

Perry sweet-talked his uncle into giving him a little traveling money and returned to Europe. Half a year in Spain, France and Algeria satisfied his wanderlust and sparked his interest in writing.

In 1931, Perry came back to the Lone Star State and married Claire Hodges, the daughter of a Beaumont doctor he had met while a student at Southwestern. The newlyweds moved into the family home with his grandmother and struggled to survive on $100 a month from the groom's inheritance.

George Sessions Perry looks like a man without a care in the world, but he was only five years away from ending his own life. *RGD5F6286, Houston Public Library, HMRC.*

Over the next six years, the aspiring author produced six novels and more than fifty short stories, all with rural Texas settings, but never got so much as a nibble from publishing houses and national magazines.

Perry surely would have given up if it had not been for the steadfast support and constant encouragement of his self-sacrificing soul mate. Claire not only translated his scrawl into neatly typed manuscripts and corrected his grammar but also stood up to her husband's dictatorial granny, something his own mother had never done.

The big break came at last in 1937. The *Saturday Evening Post* finally accepted one of Perry's submissions, and Doubleday bought his first novel, *Walls Rise Up*, the comic tale of three Brazos River vagrants. Within two years, he sold a dozen more short stories and went to Hollywood to work on a movie script.

*Hold Autumn in Your Hand*, generally considered the best depiction of agrarian life in Texas, was published in 1941. The critically acclaimed book won the Texas Institute of Letters Award and the National Book Award for the thirty-one-year-old novelist. The 1945 motion picture *The Southerner*, starring native Texan Zachary Scott, was based upon *Hold Autumn in Your Hand.*

Perry felt publicly humiliated by his rejection for military service in World War II due to a stiff elbow suffered in a fall from a horse. Determined to do his patriotic part, he went overseas as a civilian war correspondent and covered the Allied landings on Sicily in 1943.

Perry was so traumatized by the horrors of combat that he could never again bring himself to write fiction. Lighthearted yarns about the colorful folk of the Texas countryside suddenly seemed sacrilegious.

Perry managed to stay busy, however, churning out fifty-seven magazine pieces, all but a handful for the *Saturday Evening Post* and its sister periodical the *Country Gentleman*, between 1945 and 1950. Twenty-four of those articles were for the *Saturday Evening Post*'s popular Cities of America series, an ironic assignment for someone who openly despised the urban lifestyle.

In the early 1950s, Perry's output dropped to six or seven articles a year. His sole book-length project was a seventy-fifth-anniversary history of Texas A&M.

He never seemed to run out of reasons to feel guilty. His success had made it financially feasible for Claire and him to move to Connecticut in the late 1940s. But as the insightful biography in the *Handbook of Texas* explains: "Perry developed a growing sense of guilt at having abandoned his roots in rural Texas and his first love, fiction, for what he saw as the easier and more lucrative field of journalism. In terms of farming metaphors that he liked to use, he felt that he had opted for the easy 'sandy land farming' instead of the harder, but more satisfying, 'black land farming.' "

Arthritis of the spine made research and writing increasingly difficult. For years, Perry had put off seeing a doctor for the crippling condition, preferring instead to medicate himself with whiskey, and by 1954, he was an alcoholic wreck haunted by voices and hallucinations.

Four days before the tormented Texan disappeared in December 1956, the friend that later identified his body dropped by the author's Connecticut home. "The best thing I can do in this depressed state," Perry told the visitor, "is either jump into the river and swim to the north pole or run into the woods until I drop."

The two-month search for the missing writer ended on February 13, 1957, with the discovery of George Sessions Perry's body in a river not far from his Connecticut home. In death, he returned to his roots for burial in the Odd Fellows Cemetery in Rockdale, where his widow joined him eighteen years later.

32

# KATHERINE ANNE PORTER

## *A Literary Exile*

Callie Russell Porter began her long life in 1890 at a wide spot in the road not far from Brownwood called Indian Creek. She was just two when her mother died and her father took his four small children home to Kyle, between Austin and San Marcos.

For the next nine years, Catherine Anne Porter was the glue that held the motherless family together. She was the real-life inspiration for the strong women in her granddaughter's fiction and undoubtedly would have been pleased that Callie borrowed her name.

After Grandmother Porter's death in 1901, Katherine Anne Porter attended a private girls' school in San Antonio. But her formal education came to an abrupt end when she had to move to Victoria to support her unemployed father as well as her herself by giving dance, voice and dramatic lessons.

Desperate to get out of the house and away from her shiftless sire, Porter married a railroad clerk a month after turning sixteen in June 1906. Eight unhappy years later, she left husband number one and caught a train for Chicago.

Following a two-year battle with tuberculosis, Porter covered the theater and society beats for a Fort Worth newspaper. She landed a job in 1918 as a reporter with the *Rocky Mountain News* but nearly died in Denver during the influenza epidemic.

As soon as she was back on her feet and could afford the fare, Porter traveled to New York, which served as home base throughout the 1920s.

She sold her first short story in 1922 to *Century Magazine* and turned four visits to Mexico into working vacations with several articles on south-of-the-border politics and culture.

Her Roaring Twenties union with a World War I pilot from England, who was described by one biographer as "a charming rake, passive in temperament, who exasperated Porter," resulted in marriage. The knot the couple tied in 1925 was cut the next year.

Katherine Anne Porter, the first lady of Texas letters, rarely visited the Lone Star State the last sixty years of her long life. *VFBIO-PORTER, Houston Public Library, HMRC.*

While in Mexico in 1930, Porter met Eugene Pressley. They spent most of the Depression years together, the last three in Europe as husband and wife. But the relationship finally ran its course, and she returned to the United States in 1936 without her third spouse.

In May 1936, Porter made a pilgrimage with her father to her mother's weed-covered grave at Indian Creek. The melancholy reunion supposedly brought them closer together but not close enough for her to attend his funeral six years later.

The restless writer stayed on the move, living in Pennsylvania, New York, New Orleans, Houston (where she shocked relatives with rouged earlobes!) and Baton Rouge over two hectic years. She thrived on the gypsy existence, cranking out a trio of classics with Texas settings—*Noon Wine*, *Old Morality* and *The Grave*.

In 1938, Porter took her fourth and final walk down the aisle with a graduate student nearly half her age. Twenty-seven-year-old Albert Erskine believed his blushing bride was in her thirties and did not discover until his wedding day that she was actually forty-eight. Neither the groom nor the marriage ever recovered from the shock.

The trilogy *Pale Horse, Pale Rider* made Porter a big-name author in 1939. She was pleased to have her work nominated for the first Book of the Year Award from the Texas Institute of Letters but crushed when the prize went to J. Frank Dobie for *Apache Gold and Yanqui Silver*.

Porter tried to put down roots with the purchase of a home at Saratoga Springs, New York, during World War II. But a lack of cash caused her to lose the place, and she headed for Hollywood in 1945 with high hopes of making a bundle writing movie scripts. This plan, like so many others, withered on the vine.

In 1948, the financially strapped author stumbled into a new career as guest lecturer at a series of prestigious universities. For someone who had never set foot in a college classroom, the invitations from Stanford, the University of Michigan, University of Liège in Belgium and Washington and Lee were especially gratifying.

In 1968, Porter published *Ship of Fools*, her one and only novel. Reviews were mixed, but the half-million dollars she was paid for the movie rights provided the financial security she had never had.

A $600 speaking fee plus the prospect of a triumphant homecoming enticed Porter back to Texas, ending her twenty-year absence. Surprised and flattered by the enthusiastic reception, she left with warm feelings toward her estranged state.

No sooner had Porter unpacked than a letter arrived with an Austin postmark. A high-ranking administrator gave her the distinct impression that the University of Texas (UT) had decided to honor her with a library. She was thrilled beyond words and quickly wrote back with a promise to donate her papers to the project.

But it was all a misunderstanding or so said UT officials. Ground was never broken but an old woman's heart certainly was.

And that is how Katherine Anne Porter wound up next to her mother in the graveyard at Indian Creek and her papers halfway across the country at the University of Maryland. Even in death, the literary exile has not completely come home.

33

# JIM REEVES

## "Gentleman Jim"

James Travis Reeves was born in 1923 or 1924 in the northeast Texas county of Panola, the birthplace nineteen years earlier of singing cowboy Tex Ritter. Like his silver-screen predecessor, the farm boy took a precocious interest in music and was warbling on the radio by the age of ten.

In high school, however, baseball became Jim Reeves's first love as he matured into a six-foot-two, 185-pound pitcher with a greased-lightning fastball. His deeds on the diamond earned a scholarship to the University of Texas in 1942 and soon afterward a professional opportunity with the St. Louis Cardinals. But a leg injury crippled a promising career in only his second minor-league season.

The washed-up athlete returned to radio as a disc jockey in Henderson, where he sang on the side to supplement his meager income. Five years of relative obscurity ended with a sudden summons from KWKH, the Shreveport station that broadcast *Louisiana Hayride.*

Although Reeves acted as master of ceremonies for the live show, he occasionally filled in for absent guests. Substituting for self-destructive Hank Williams one night in 1953, he so impressed a record company executive who happened to be in the audience, that he was signed to a contract the moment the program went off the air.

Reeves's second release, a catchy tune called "Mexican Joe," soared to the top of the country music charts, as did "Bimbo" a short time later. But the skeptical sensation hesitated to give up his steady job in Shreveport for fear his overnight success might turn into a short-lived fluke.

After considerable coaxing, he reluctantly took a leave of absence from the *Louisiana Hayride* to go on a cross-country tour. To his astonishment, every appearance was a standing-room-only sellout.

On the heels of the singing safari, Reeves switched to a major record label and stepped in as the summer replacement for Red Foley on the television show *Ozark Jubilee*. Then in late 1955, he joined the star-studded cast of the *Grand Ole Opry*.

Reeves proved he had real staying power with a remarkable forty-six Top Ten hits in barely a decade. His string of smash singles included "Four Walls," "A Touch of Velvet," "Guilty," "Blue Canadian Rockies," "Tahiti," "Heartbreak in Silhouette," "Golden Memories and Silver Tears," "I Could Cry," "I'll Follow You" and the all-time favorite "He'll Have to Go," which sold over three million copies in 1960.

The demands of his unparalleled popularity kept "Gentleman Jim" on the road 275 days a year. To squeeze more time out his hectic schedule for his family in Tennessee, he became a licensed pilot.

But the amateur aviator recognized the risk in the constant cloud hopping, as a prophetic comment in May 1964 clearly revealed: "The main trouble and danger with tours is getting there and back."

Marty Robbins stepped onto the porch of his home on the wooded outskirts of Nashville for a better look at a violent summer thunderstorm on July 31, 1964. Although the overcast sky concealed the craft, he heard the sickening sputter of the engine followed by the unmistakable sound of the small plane plunging to earth. "Somebody's been killed out there!" he shouted in horror.

Chet Atkins, Eddy Arnold and Ernest Tubb joined Robbins and seven hundred volunteers in the difficult search for the missing aircraft and the celebrated pilot. Forty-eight hours later, they stumbled upon the wreckage in thick underbrush a mere hundred yards from a residence.

Arnold shouldered the heavy burden of identifying the two bodies at the crash site. He confirmed with a perfunctory nod the deaths of Jim Reeves and his pianist, Dean Manuel.

The tragedy stunned the country music world, fans and performers alike, who were still mourning the loss of their favorite songstress; just sixteen months earlier, Patsy Cline also had perished in a plane crash.

Despite his premature passing, Reeves's music has never died. Thanks to his widow, who had the foresight to preserve his unreleased material, and the marvels of modern engineering, he had six posthumous number one hits. In fact, "Gentleman Jim" and Patsy Cline came back from the grave in the 1980s to sing a ghostly duet.

On a highway outside Carthage are Jim Reeves's resting place and a life-size stone likeness atop a fourteen-ton granite base. The inscription reads, "If I, a lowly singer, dry one tear or soothe one humble heart in pain, then my homely verse to God is dear, and not one stanza has been sung in vain."

34

# TEX RITTER

## *Law's Loss Country Music's Gain*

Woodward Maurice Ritter was born on January 11, 1905, deep in the piney woods of East Texas in an out-of-the-way village called Murvaul. Besides the finest voice in the musically gifted family, he also had the sharpest mind.

Graduating at the head of his high school class in Beaumont, he obliged his parents by taking prelaw courses at the University of Texas (UT). But cowboy ballads, not jurisprudence, fascinated the talented baritone. Exposure to Lone Star historian J. Frank Dobie, folk music scholar John A. Lomax and composer Oscar J. Fox, all members of the UT faculty, convinced the undergraduate he was not cut out for the courtroom.

Ritter finally scratched his showbiz itch in 1928 and dropped out of college to join the male chorus of a traveling troupe. Winding up in New York that November with ten cents in his pocket, the Texan enjoyed a Thanksgiving dinner of a plateful of greasy French fries.

The struggling singer's big break came two years later with a role in the Broadway production of *Green Grow the Lilacs*. Going by the northern nickname of "Tex," he was soon swamped with radio and record offers.

For five hectic years, Ritter was a celebrity on the Manhattan airwaves. His three radio programs—*Tex Ritter's Campfire*, *WHN Barn Dance* and *Cowboy Tom's Roundup*—consistently chalked up sky-high ratings.

Ritter enjoyed similar success in his 1933 debut as a recording artist. Both sides of his premier single, "Rye Whiskey" and the sentimental "Good-bye, Old Paint," were huge hits.

Hollywood beckoned in 1936, when Grand National Pictures settled on Ritter as the answer to Gene Autry at rival Republic. Astride his mount White Flash, Tex rode off into a dozen sunsets in less than two years before the shoestring studio closed its doors.

Ritter landed on his feet at Monogram Pictures, where he cranked out twenty lyrical Westerns. (He made four of those flicks with actress Dorothy Fay, who became his wife in 1941.) Since the formula was more important than the plot, he often finished a whole day's shooting without ever glancing at the script.

On the strength of his box-office appeal as one of the silver screen's top ten attractions, Ritter jumped to Columbia. This supposedly smart career move to a major studio turned out to be a serious mistake, as he wound up playing second fiddle to Bill Elliot.

Ritter swallowed his disappointment and honored the nine-feature commitment with Columbia. Free at last to resume his search for greener cinematic pastures, he temporarily hung his hat at Universal only to be overshadowed by the resident sagebrush star Johnny Mack Brown.

Ritter's fifth stop on his decade-long tour of Hollywood was PRC Pictures, where he appeared in the memorable Texas Rangers series. The end of the Second World War coincided with the release of his eighty-fifth and final film.

Even though the movies failed to live up to his high expectations, the low-budget features had earned him a large and loyal following. Zealous fans in every corner of the country loved his distinctive vocals and waited in long lines to hear him perform in person.

Ritter was composer Dimitri Tiomkin's choice to record his title tune for a new Western costarring Gary Cooper and Grace Kelly. Both the motion picture and the song were fabulous favorites, and Tex sang "High Noon" at the 1953 Academy Awards ceremony.

By 1960, Ritter was spending most of his time in Nashville, the emerging capital of country music. He served two consecutive terms as president of the Country Music Association and in 1964 was elected to the Country Music Hall of Fame, the first artist so honored in his lifetime.

During the turmoil of the late 1960s, Ritter took a political detour to the far right. Egged on by misguided friends and ultraconservative zealots, the wealthy novice sought the Republican nomination for a Tennessee seat in the U.S. Senate. He spent a fortune on the expensive campaign but won barely a fifth of the primary vote.

Ten days before his sixty-ninth birthday in 1974, Ritter received a late-night phone call from the Nashville police station. A musician in his band

With his broad smile and rich baritone, it was easy to like Tex Ritter. *RGD5F407, Houston Public Library, HMRC.*

had been arrested on child support charges and lacked the cold cash to make bail.

Never one to turn his back on a friend in need, the country music legend dressed and drove down to the city jail. As the bond papers were being drawn up, he suddenly clutched his chest and fell to the floor.

Ritter was dead, the victim of a massive coronary. The heart as big as his native Texas had simply given out.

Ritter's son John, of *Three's Company* fame, also died of a heart condition and at an even younger age—fifty-four.

If the voice of Big Al, the fattest bear in the Country Bear Jamboree at Disneyworld, sounds familiar, it should. That is Tex Ritter doing the talking.

35

# GINGER ROGERS

## *Famed Dancer Won Acting Oscar*

Fourteen-year-old Ginger Rogers danced circles around the competition at the Baker Hotel in Dallas on November 9, 1925, to win first place in the state Charleston contest.

Virginia Katherine McMath was born in Independence, Missouri—Harry Truman's hometown—but like most "naturalized" Texans came to the Lone Star State just as soon as she could. In the case of Ginger, a nickname from a cousin who could not pronounce "Virginia," it was in 1922 at the age of eleven when she moved to Fort Worth with her mother and stepfather, John Rogers.

Ginger's mother, a former movie scriptwriter, took a job as theater critic for a Cow Town newspaper. Her daughter's formal education ended three years later with her first-place finish in the state Charleston contest. The fourteen-year-old's prize was a six-month vaudeville contract.

Three years later, the teenager was half of a song-and-dance act billed as "Ginger and Pepper" with the first of her five husbands. Her marriage to Edward "Jack Pepper" Culpepper did not last the year, and the young divorcée resumed her solo career under the protective wing of her savvy mother.

They jumped off the vaudeville merry-go-round in New York, where Rogers found work singing on the radio. That left her ample time for auditions, and she soon landed a part in the Broadway musical *Top Speed*, which opened on Christmas Day 1929.

The talented Texan made such a profound impression on George and Ira Gershwin that the brothers chose her for the leading role in their new

Ginger Rogers and Fred Astaire danced their way into movie audiences' hearts in the 1930s and 1940s. *RGD5F2164A, Houston Public Library, HMRC.*

musical. In a few whirlwind weeks, *Girl Crazy* made nineteen-year-old Ginger Rogers the brightest star on Broadway.

Happy as she was with her overnight success on the Great White Way, Rogers, with her mother's enthusiastic blessing, saw New York as merely the launch pad for a career in motion pictures. Deciding time was of the essence, they moved to Hollywood at the peak of the promising performer's stage success.

In three hectic years, Rogers made twenty-two feature films for six different studios. Her selection as one of fifteen "Baby Stars" signaled her official arrival in Tinsel Town.

Then in 1933, in what proved to be a studio-saving stroke of genius, RKO paired Rogers, all of twenty-two at the time, with Fred Astaire, thirty-four, for *Flying Down to Rio*. The dream couple danced their way into America's heart and in the process, to quote a movie historian, "revolutionized the Hollywood musical, introducing dance routines of unprecedented elegance and virtuosity, set to songs specially composed for them by the greatest song composers of the day."

RKO, as well as its box-office attractions, knew a good thing when they saw it, namely the ticket sales. As a result, eight more Ginger-and-Fred vehicles packed theaters from coast to coast between 1934 and 1939. MGM persuaded the duo to work their magic one last time in their 1949 reunion, *The Barkleys of Broadway*.

Astaire had nothing but the highest praise for his beautiful partner: "All the girls I ever danced with thought they couldn't do it, but of course they could. So they always cried. All except Ginger. No, no, Ginger never cried."

To that tribute to her toughness, he graciously added, "Ginger was brilliantly effective. She made everything work for her. Actually she made things very fine for the both of us and she deserves most of the credit for our success."

During the decade between her ninth and final on-screen collaboration with Astaire, Rogers established herself as a dramatic actress of the highest order. Her outstanding title-role performance in *Kitty Foyle* earned her the 1941 Academy Award for Best Actress.

Her Oscar gave Rogers the clout to break out of the studio system, an unprecedented act of rebellion in those days. Once again, Lela Rogers showed she was much more than a parasitic "stage mother" by helping her only child chart an independent course in the shark-infested waters of Hollywood.

By the mid-1950s, however, Rogers's big-screen career was coming to a close. Parts for middle-aged actresses were few and far between, and she made only five of her seventy-three films after 1955.

Determined to prove she was far from over the hill, Rogers returned to the New York stage. She played to rave reviews and packed houses in long-running productions of *Hello, Dolly!* and *Mame*.

Rogers took the latter musical to London in 1969 to the delight of British playgoers and the queen, who requested a Royal Command Performance. The American icon left fourteen months later as the highest-paid performer in the history of the West End theater district.

Rogers's personal life did not measure up to her public accomplishments. She went through five marriages, with none lasting more than eight years. After showing her final husband the door in 1969, she did not walk down the aisle again.

Ginger Rogers passed away in 1995 at her California home. In her eighty-three years, the Christian Scientist had never visited a doctor or set foot in a hospital.

36

# ZACHARY SCOTT

## *Why Austin Theater Called "The Zach"*

Zachary Thomson Scott Jr. was born in Austin in 1914. The surgeon's son was expected to follow in his father's footsteps but never showed any interest in medicine. He was drawn instead to drama and began appearing in plays while still in high school.

At the University of Texas, Zach Scott combined acting and athletics. He landed leading roles in several college productions as well as the presidency of the Curtain Club while at the same time running track.

Deciding to see the world, Scott dropped out of college and worked his way to Europe on a freighter. During an extended stay in London, he joined a repertory company and gained invaluable theatrical experience on the English stage.

Scott came home in 1935 and on his twenty-first birthday married his college sweetheart, Elaine Anderson, whose family also had money. The newlyweds lived in New York for a short spell but returned to Austin so the young husband could finish college.

Scott burned the candle at both ends holding down two jobs—director of the Little Theater and drama teacher at St. Mary's Academy—while carrying a full course load. After graduation in 1939, the couple again pulled up stakes for Manhattan with the blessing and financial backing of both sets of parents.

With his lean good looks, natural charisma and talent, Scott found plenty of work on Broadway. Elaine, on the other hand, could not get her foot in the door and eventually settled for a behind-the-scenes career in production.

Zachary Scott sure looked the part of a villainous cad, the reason why he played so many in the movies. *RGD5F6485, Houston Public Library, HMRC.*

None other than Jack Warner himself, of Warner Bros. Studio, discovered Scott in 1943. Due to the wartime shortage of matinee idols, the movie mogul at once signed the twenty-nine-year-old Texan to a long-term contract and put him right to work.

As a mysterious international criminal in the suspense classic *The Mask of Dimitrios*, Scott holds his own opposite screen veterans Peter Lorre and Sidney Greenstreet. More than seven decades later, his first motion picture is still between-the-wars intrigue at its best, thanks to an outstanding cast and a superb story.

Scott followed this auspicious debut with what most critics and fans consider his finest performance. In *The Southerner*, the film adaptation of Texan George Sessions Perry's award-winning novel *Hold Autumn in Your Hand*, the rich kid proves he could truly act with a convincing portrayal of a struggling sharecropper.

With just two movies under his belt, Scott looked like he was on the fast track to stardom. In the 1946 "Stars of Tomorrow" poll, he came in third, ahead of Eve Arden, Yvonne De Carlo and Robert Mitchum. The reviewer for his hometown paper called him "Austin's one contribution and perhaps Texas' most distinguished gift to the motion picture industry."

In the newcomer's third feature, released in 1946, he plays Joan Crawford's "rotter of a second husband" in *Mildred Pierce*. Scott gives a credible performance but is overshadowed not only by the scene-stealing star but also by Eve Arden and Ann Blyth, both of whom received Academy Award nominations for Best Supporting Actress.

In those days, an actor was studio property and did what he was told, no questions asked. When Humphrey Bogart balked at doing the mediocre Western *Stallion Rock* for another studio in 1947, Scott filled in for him on loan from Warner Bros.

He seemed to get back in the groove playing a poor youth willing to sacrifice anything and anybody for wealth and power in the rags-to-riches melodrama *Ruthless*. But that part and similar roles in pictures like *The Unfaithful* and *Cass Timberlane* typecast him as a cad, villain and all-around bad guy.

Scott's 1949 reunion with Joan Crawford, also a Texas native, should have given his career a boost, but *Flamingo Road* turned out to be his last major motion picture. It did not help that he shaved his trademark mustache and played a spineless deputy sheriff.

When Scott went to Hollywood, Elaine stayed in New York, and in 1950, they made the separation permanent. She wasted no time in marrying famous author John Steinbeck, and he later wed actress Ruth Ford.

Roles were fewer and farther between for Scott in the 1950s, and the quality of the movies steadily declined. He made his final film, a Jerry Lewis comedy, in 1962 and returned to his first love—the stage.

The Scotts were giving readings of William Faulkner's works at the University of Mississippi in the winter of 1965, when Zach took to bed seriously ill. The lifelong smoker was diagnosed with lung cancer, and the disease was destined for his brain. He spent his last weeks at the family home in Austin, where he died that October at age fifty-one.

Seven years later, the Austin Community Theater needed money for a new stage. Zachary Scott's sister made a six-figure contribution on condition the theater would be renamed for her brother. She never imagined that, in keeping with the flippant familiarity so common in Austin, it would someday be called "The Zach."

37

# ANN SHERIDAN

## The "Oomph" Girl

The Sheridans, of Denton, Texas, brought their fifth and final child into their modest home on February 21, 1915, and gave the baby girl the name Clara Lou.

Looking back on her formative years in the North Texas town, the self-described "tomboy" once recalled with unmistakable pride, "I can whistle through my fingers, bulldog a steer, light a fire with two sticks and shoot a pistol with fair accuracy." She also played basketball well enough to make the women's team at the local college. Not the usual skill set for one of the most glamorous actresses of Hollywood's "golden age."

Sheridan was a seventeen-year-old student at North Texas State Teachers College when her sister Pauline secretly entered her sibling with the head-turning looks in Paramount's "Search for Beauty" contest. The attractive teenager won the competition and the first prize, which included a movie contract and a cameo in the motion picture *Search for Beauty*. It introduced the Texas coed to the world.

Sheridan quit school, moved to California and went to work in 1934 at Paramount Studios as a $75-a-week contract extra. The moviemakers kept the new hire busy casting her in fourteen films that first year alone. All the roles were tiny bit parts with only a couple of words of dialogue and often with no on-screen credit.

"Clara Lou" was a mite too country for the studio snobs' taste, but they could not settle on a stage name for their new property. She became Ann Sheridan purely by accident after playing a character by that name in an

Ann Sheridan showed in this 1952 photograph that she still had plenty of "oomph" at age thirty-seven. *RGD5F610.b, Houston Public Library, HMRC.*

on-lot production put on by her drama coach. Everyone, even the obliging young starlet, agreed she looked like an "Ann."

Things began to look up for Sheridan after a director insisted upon giving her a speaking role in the film *Behold My Wife*. Impressed by her rock-solid performance, especially in an emotional suicide scene, Paramount extended her contract.

The size and scope of her roles improved for awhile. She was chosen for the female lead opposite Fred MacMurray in the 1935 flick *Car 99*, followed by a Western with Randolph Scott titled *Rocky Mountain Mystery*. But by the end of the year, she was back to one-line parts—the prelude to Paramount's decision to let her go.

Sheridan was not in the unemployment line for long, though. She signed with Warner Bros. and soon was making better movies, a combined total of eighteen in 1937 and 1938, with box-office mainstays like Humphrey Bogart, Pat O'Brien and Dick Powell.

She stepped up to Warner Bros.' "top tier" with the female lead in the hit crime drama *Angels with Dirty Faces*, released in November 1938. Her name appeared alongside James Cagney and Humphrey Bogart on movie theater marquees across the country.

Warner's publicity department shifted into high gear with a campaign to make Ann Sheridan a topic of kitchen table conversation. To give her a slightly scandalous image, she was touted as "The Oomph Girl" and ordered to show her face in Hollywood nightclubs at least three evenings a week.

Sheridan hated that nickname but wisely kept her opinion to herself. Years later, she had second thoughts, saying, "If it hadn't been for 'oomph,' I'd probably still be in the chorus."

"I was struck by her extraordinary magnetism and directness," English icon Rex Harrison said of "The Oomph Girl." He recognized in her that "distinctive quality of earthiness that never transcends to blatant sexiness."

Sheridan finally found stardom during the war years of the 1940s with a deft mixture of comedies like *It All Came True*, *Navy Blues* and *The Man Who Came to Dinner* and taut dramas such as *Torrid Zone*, *They Drive by Night* and *Kings Row*, which features her most critically acclaimed performance as well as future president Ronald Reagan at his best.

Nonetheless, by the late 1940s, Sheridan's career in motion pictures was in irreversible decline. Warner Bros. lost interest in the aging actress, even though she was still in her thirties, and pushed her out the door. Work for the freelance performer was hard to come by in Hollywood, so she switched coasts in search of greener pastures in the New York–centered television industry.

Sheridan's long relationship with publicist Steve Hannagan, which had followed her two brief marriages, ended with his sudden death in 1953. She took the loss hard but eventually picked up the pieces of her life and career with an occasional movie, stage show tours and better luck in television, which included a year on the soap opera *Another World*.

Sheridan's career—as well as her personal life—was on the rebound by 1966. She was happily married to her third husband and starring in her own successful television show, *Pistols and Petticoats*.

Then on January 21, 1967, Ann Sheridan died at her California home from cancer of the esophagus and liver at the age of fifty-one. Not a single person, even her spouse, knew she had been terminally ill for months.

38

# AARON SPELLING

## "Big Tex" His Neighbor

Aaron Spelling, the biggest big shot in the history of television, was born in Dallas to poor immigrant parents in April 1923. An Ellis Island clerk changed his father's name from Spurling to Spelling the day the Polish Jew entered the country. The new arrival found a Russian-born mate with the same ethnic roots and moved halfway across the continent to Texas.

Spelling grew up in a small frame house down the street from Fair Park that was not built for a family of six. Reflecting on the poverty of his upbringing, he revealed in a 1996 interview: "I still have nightmares about being in a $6,000 home in Dallas, Texas. Wall-to-wall people (and) one bathroom. I was the one to go to the local bakery a block away on Saturday to get the day-old stuff."

The skinny kid hated school, where bigger boys took pleasure in picking on him. Trauma from the verbal and physical abuse caused him to lose the use of his legs at age eight and to spend a whole year in bed.

Spelling ultimately went back to class and, like Stanley Marcus of Neiman Marcus fame before him, graduated from Forest Avenue High School. He enlisted in the Army Air Corps in 1942 and spent most of World War II putting on plays for the troops.

The Texan did not, however, spend the entire war far from enemy lines. A sniper shot him in a hand, leaving a wound that never healed completely. For that injury, he was compensated with the Bronze Star and Purple Heart.

The young veteran returned to Dallas and attended his hometown college, Southern Methodist University, on the GI Bill. Journalism was his major, but the drama department took up most of his free time as he learned to act and to write plays. And just for fun, he led cheers for the SMU football team and Heisman Trophy winner Doak Walker.

The first thing Spelling did after obtaining his diploma in 1949 was to depart Dallas for the bright lights of Broadway. But his high hopes of making it as a wet-behind-the-ears playwright were quickly brought down to earth.

Instead of diminishing his ambition, the disappointment only changed his career plan. Confident in his acting ability, he headed for the opposite coast, hungry for any role Hollywood casting directors might offer.

Lacking the looks of the stereotypical leading man, Spelling had to settle for quirky and villainous bit parts. He found plenty of work, appearing in forty television shows and a dozen movies, but in 1953 decided his future was behind the camera and not in front of it.

That was also the year Spelling married an actress from Amarillo by the name of Carolyn Jones. The beautiful brunette could pick and choose her parts, and the one she accepted in *The Bachelor Party* landed her a 1957 Academy Award nomination for Best Supporting Actress.

Meanwhile, Spelling was starting to get the hang of scriptwriting thanks to his friend and mentor Dick Powell, who hired him to crank out small-screen stories for *Zane Grey Theater*. This break blossomed into an even bigger opportunity in 1959, when Powell promoted him to producer.

Aaron Spelling hammed it up in his cheerleading days at Southern Methodist University. *1949 SMU Rotunda Yearbook, Houston Public Library, HMRC.*

*Burke's Law*, starring Gene Barry as a millionaire crime fighter, was Spelling's ice-breaker in 1963, and he followed the Golden Globe winner in 1965 with the equally popular *Honey West*, with Anne Francis.

The Spellings' marriage had ended in divorce the previous year. Carolyn went on to her most memorable performance, as Morticia in the television comedy *The Addams Family*, before her death in 1983.

Following the death of Dick Powell, Spelling formed a production company with entertainer Danny Thomas. The highlight of their four-year collaboration was *The Mod Squad*, nominated six years running for the top-drama Emmy.

Spelling hit his stride in the 1970s with *The Rookies*, *Starsky and Hutch*, *S.W.A.T.*, *Charlie's Angels*, *The Love Boat*, *Fantasy Island*, *Vega$* and *Hart to Hart*. Under exclusive contract to ABC, the producer with the magic touch was responsible for a third of the network's prime-time programming by the end of the decade.

Speaking of detractors that dismissed his successful shows as "mindless candy," Spelling once said, "The knocks by the critics bother you. But you have a choice of proving yourself to 300 critics or 30 million fans."

Spelling's after-dark soap opera *Dynasty* defined television-watching in the 1980s. At the end of its nine-season run, the ABC executives showed their appreciation for all he had done by refusing to renew his contract. But he bounced right back with hit programs for the new Fox network.

Before his death in 2006 from complications following a stroke, Aaron Spelling could be seen waving to busloads of tourists from the driveway of his 56,500-square-foot California mansion. Sure, it was ostentatious and over the top, but it was a way for the skinny, insecure kid from Fair Park to show the world how far he had come.

39

# KING VIDOR

## *Genius behind the Camera*

The Galveston native, who survived the 1900 hurricane as a boy of six, was mesmerized by the newfangled medium called "the movies." Landing a part-time job at a local theater, he spent countless hours watching the screen spring to life with thrilling tales of faraway places.

To the young Texan, picture shows were pure magic, and soon his heart was set on becoming a behind-the-scenes sorcerer. Although Vidor's first attempts at homemade cinema, an amateurish recreation of the Great Storm and live footage of troops on maneuver, were nothing special, his simple story of a seaside car race showed real promise.

With his future wife, the beautiful Florence Arto, in the starring role, *In Tow* enjoyed modest success at movie houses throughout southeast Texas. Rushing to New York to peddle his pride and joy, Vidor was swindled by an unscrupulous distributor who stole his money and vanished with the only copy of the film.

Unfazed by the setback, Vidor and his new bride set off for California in a Model T Ford in 1915. Arriving six weeks later with a shriveled nest egg of a dollar and twenty cents, the couple lived on secondhand food scrounged from grocery store trash bins before finally finding work.

While Florence got in on the ground floor as a bit player, Vidor doggedly cranked out screenplays, writing a grand total of fifty-two before his first sale. To make ends meet, he labored as a nameless extra for a buck and a half a day plus lunch.

When Universal offered him a clerical position at the stupendous salary of twelve dollars a week, Vidor jumped at the chance for a steady paycheck. He soon graduated to scripting comedies for the immortal Mack Sennett and his slapstick crew, including the Keystone Kops, Charlie Chaplin, Ben Turpin and Mabel Normand.

Following a sudden layoff at Universal in 1918, Vidor became an independent producer not so much by choice but out of necessity. Financed by a group of California doctors, he completed a melodrama with, strangely enough, a strong Christian Science message. *The Turn in the Road* cost a modest $9,000 but grossed over $365,000.

Vidor satisfied the physicians' demand for more of the same with three similar movies in a hectic seven months. Foolishly investing his last penny in Vidor Village, his own short-lived studio, he published a lofty "Creed and Pledge" in *Variety*, which proclaimed in part: "So long as I direct pictures, I will make only those founded upon principles of right, and I will endeavor to draw upon the inexhaustible source of good for my stories, my guidance and my inspiration."

Five years later, Vidor made his mark with *The Big Parade*, a silent-era classic. A smash hit at the box office as well as with the critics, the brutally honest depiction of World War I combat established John Gilbert as a 1920s matinee idol and Metro-Goldwyn-Mayer as a major studio. The picture earned an amazing $15 million, but the director made a $3 million mistake by giving up his twenty percent share for a pittance.

Vidor followed *The Big Parade* with the highly acclaimed *La Bohéme*, featuring Lillian Gish. In preparation for the famous death scene, the great actress drank no liquids for three days and mastered a mysterious technique for imperceptible breathing. Her moving performance reduced everyone on the set to tears and caused Vidor to marvel, "The movies have never known a more dedicated artist."

In spite of his well-intentioned "Creed" and silent achievements, Vidor fathered several talking turkeys. Maybe the worst was a 1932 bomb made to order for David O. Selznick, who insisted upon casting Delores Del Rio opposite Joel McCrea in a South Seas romance. "I don't care what story you use," said the studio head, "so long as we call it *Bird of Paradise* and Del Rio jumps into a flaming volcano at the finish."

Vidor's twenty-seven sound films were by no means all B-movie embarrassments. The best of the bunch were *Hallelujah* (1929), *Billy the Kid* (1930), *The Champ* (1931), *Our Daily Bread* (1934), *The Citadel* (1938, it earned an Academy Award nomination), *Northwest Passage* (1940) and *The Fountainhead* (1949).

King Vidor is in the *Guinness Book of World Records* for the longest directing career in film history—sixty-seven years. *RGD5-B001-F0024-601, Houston Public Library, HMRC.*

Wrapping up his fifty-fourth and final feature in 1959, Vidor reluctantly retired. After four decades behind the camera, his exit was less a voluntary departure than tacit admission decent scripts were no longer coming his way.

Vidor spent his last years pursuing the perfect picture for a comeback. With the unsolved 1922 murder of fellow director William Desmond Taylor, he found the ideal vehicle. But the shocking identity of the killer caused him to shelve the project shortly before his death in 1982.

As much as he wanted to get back on top, King Vidor could not bring himself to put on the screen the true story of a Hollywood homicide that went unpunished.

40

# DAVID WESTHEIMER

## Ex-POW Wrote Best Seller

Anyone who has ever driven the streets of Texas's largest city has at one time or another crossed Westheimer Road. Few realize, however, that the urban thoroughfare named for a nineteenth-century German immigrant is the longest in the entire Lone Star State.

Mitchell Louis Westheimer came to Texas in the 1850s. A huge success at every enterprise he tried, the businessman, who spoke seven languages, and his wife raised a houseful of children—eight of their own, three orphans and five more belonging to struggling relatives.

One of Westheimer's many descendants was great-nephew David Westheimer. Born in the Bayou City in 1917, he graduated from Rice Institute at age twenty and joined the staff of the *Houston Post*. He was juggling the dual duties of editor and columnist by the time the United States entered the Second World War and in short order put his civilian life on hold to enlist in the Army Air Forces.

On the morning of December 11, 1942, a B-24 Liberator with the unwieldy name *Natchez to Mobile, Memphis to St. Jo*, inspired by the comic strip *Li'l Abner*, lumbered into the air from a field on the Suez Canal. The target of the day was the port of Naples eight hundred miles to the northwest on the coast of Italy.

The young lieutenant from Texas was one of eight crewmen on board the four-engine bomber. It was Westheimer's twenty-ninth mission and, unbeknownst to him, his last. He was about to be grounded for the duration.

When the *Houston Post* ran this photograph of its former editor and columnist in 1943, David Westheimer had been a POW for six months. *RGD5F6247, Houston Public Library, HMRC.*

The best-selling novelist waited more than forty years to write his wartime memoir, aptly titled *Sitting It Out.* But time had taken not the slightest toll on his recollection of the day his B-24 went down, which he described in riveting detail.

"We dropped our load and continued out to sea," Westheimer wrote in 1992. "I gave Lt. Larry Kennedy, the pilot, the course for home. And then we were jumped by Macchi 202s. Italy's frontline fighters."

Westheimer immediately manned one of the .50-caliber guns in the nose of the plane. "I never got off a burst," he admitted. "The Macchis were in and out too quickly for me."

Crew members not tied up tending to wounded comrades kept trying to fend off the swarming fighters, but the bomber suffered serious damage despite their best efforts.

An oil leak caused an engine to freeze up, starting a devastating domino effect: "That tore number three right out of the wing. It fell into number four, knocking it out of the wing, too. I looked out the Plexiglass window into two gaping holes where the engines had been."

The sudden loss of half its power sealed the fate of the *Natchez to Mobile, Memphis to St. Jo.* "We were losing altitude steadily. It was obvious we'd never make it back to the desert" was Westheimer's matter-of-fact recollection of that sobering moment.

"I started figuring an alternate course to Malta, the nearest friendly territory. I gave that up when Kennedy (the pilot)…said he couldn't maintain altitude and was going to land on the beach."

But the coastline was too narrow to accommodate the crippled bomber. The pilot was forced to ditch the B-24 in the blue water of the Mediterranean several hundred yards from shore.

Able-bodied airmen managed to pull their injured companions to safety before the aircraft sank beneath the waves. They treaded water only a few minutes before being taken prisoner by a single Italian policeman and a couple of fishermen in a rowboat.

"We were the first American bomber shot down attacking Italy and maybe the first ever shot down by Italian fighters," Westheimer wrote with a hint of embarrassment. "To paraphrase Mark Twain, given a choice, we probably would have declined the honor."

U.S troops liberated the German prisoner-of-war camp on April 29, 1945, bringing to an end the twenty-eight-month ordeal of the Houston newspaperman turned bomber navigator.

During his prolonged captivity, Westheimer thought he might become a farmer after the war, an odd daydream for a city slicker. Instead he chose writing and produced *Summer on the Water*, a work of fiction that won the McMurray Book Store prize for the best Texas first novel of 1948.

He returned to the *Houston Post* in the 1950s as an editor and sometime columnist. On the writing front, he ground out suspense novels under the pseudonym Z.Z. Smith while finishing his next novel, *Watching Out for Dulie*, which was not as well received as his first.

But the 1960s proved to be his breakthrough decade. His World War II thriller, *Von Ryan's Express*, was the February 1964 Book-of-the-Month Club selection and later made into a major motion picture starring Frank Sinatra. His next novel, *My Sweet Charlie* (1965), sold almost as many copies before he adapted the story for the Broadway stage. Previously in 1963, he had reversed the process by turning the motion picture *Days of Wine and Roses* into a novel.

David Westheimer continued to write right up until the end of his long life. His final novel, *Delay en Route*, came out in 2002, three years before his death from a heart attack at the age of eighty-eight.

41

# "BIG BOY" WILLIAMS

## Haunted by Will Rogers's Ghost

Guinn Williams Jr. was born in 1899 at the North Texas town of Decatur. He came home from the First World War in 1919 to find that his father, an influential banker and cattleman, had obtained an appointment for him to the U.S. Military Academy.

"I figured that I had already made second lieutenant and to go to West Point and work my butt off just to become a second lieutenant again seemed kind of silly," the younger Williams explained in an interview years later. "So I told my father I'd sooner play baseball and that I had an offer from the Chicago White Sox."

Junior left home, and Senior entered politics. The son learned that being the best baseball player in Decatur did not make him a major-league prospect and fell back on his ranch skills to earn a living on the rodeo circuit. The father won election to the Texas Senate followed by five terms as a congressman.

Guinn Jr., who went by Tex at the time, wandered west to Hollywood, arriving with $2.50 in his britches. Coming upon a film company shooting an outdoor scene and a laborer listlessly digging a hole, he had a brilliant idea.

"I said, 'Say! Would you lend me your pick for just a minute?' The fellow was glad to hand it to me and I tore into that hole like nobody's business. Pretty soon everybody began to watch me. They thought it was funny that anybody could be so enthusiastic about digging." Williams was hired on the spot as a stuntman.

With his wavy brown hair, gray-green eyes and muscular build, it was only a matter of time until the handsome Texan was in front of the camera. Will Rogers chose him for bit parts in three comedies the popular humorist produced out of his own pocket. The Oklahoman also dubbed the youngster "Big Boy," a catchy nickname inspired by his size—six feet two inches and two hundred-plus pounds.

As an authentic cowboy instead of the drugstore variety, Williams decided he deserved the starring role in sagebrush sagas. Although he landed the lead in *The Jack Riders* in 1921, he soon wound up trapped in so-called B-Westerns as a supporting actor.

After having an unsuccessful go at moviemaking, Williams accepted his typecast fate and made the most of it. He developed his trademark "puzzled squint," which he used with equal effectiveness as a dimwitted cowhand or a tenderhearted tough guy.

As Williams's career picked up steam in the mid-1920s, he shared the screen with four-legged performers Rex, "King of the Wild Horses," and Wolfheart, a Rin-Tin-Tin wannabe. His athletic appearance and aptitude occasionally got him out of the Western rut with parts in sports pictures like *Brown of Harvard*, *Slide Kelly Slide*, *Forward Pass* and *Big Fight*.

Even though he was one of the busiest actors in Tinsel Town, appearing in at least seventy-six pictures between 1921 and 1935, Williams always made time for Will Rogers. The twenty-year difference in their ages did not keep the two from becoming the best of friends.

"Big Boy" was a charter member of Rogers's fun-loving inner circle. Williams never asked where they were going or when they would be back when Rogers picked him up in his Pierce Arrow. All he knew for sure was that everyone was bound to have a good time.

The folksy comedian introduced Williams to polo, the rich man's game that became his passion. The dirt field on Rogers's ranch was the scene of many rough-and-tumble matches featuring the host's cowboy cronies, serious polo players and motion picture royalty like Walt Disney, Hal Roach, Darryl Zanuck and Spencer Tracy.

Hard-riding "Big Boy" was the best of the Hollywood participants. He was, in fact, a world-class polo player known as the Babe Ruth of the sport.

The tragic death of Will Rogers in a 1935 plane crash shocked all Americans, but no one took it harder than "Big Boy." He never seemed to come to terms with the loss.

Williams made no bones about the fact that movies were for him an overpaid means to an end that included a 125 polo ponies and a 5,500-acre ranch in South Texas. "I worked all the time, twelve pictures a year, but I hated every one of them. I never studied a script. I'd glance over my part just before a scene and bluff it through. I lived to drink and play polo."

When the movie studios started calling less often in the 1950s, "Big Boy" switched to the small screen. He was a cast member of two early television series, playing the village blacksmith in *My Friend Flicka* and Pete the canvas boss in *Circus Boy*.

In his next to last movie, Williams appeared as one of Jim Bowie's volunteers in the 1960 version of *The Alamo*. Two years later, he had just finished a pilot for a new show called *Button and Bows* when Joel McCrea paid him a visit. The actor was surprised to find his old friend, who should have been on top of the world, down in the dumps.

"The last three nights I have been dreaming about Will Rogers," Williams said. "He is riding Soapsuds, and he says, 'Come on, Big Boy, get on your horse and go with me!' "

"I don't feel good, Joel. It's like he was calling me."

Less than a week later, Guinn "Big Boy" Williams died of uremic poisoning at sixty-two.

42

# BOB WILLS

## *King of Western Swing*

Bob Wills was inducted into the Country Music Hall of Fame on October 18, 1968, an ironic honor since the "King of Western Swing" never thought there was anything "country" about his sound.

The first of John and Emmaline Wills' ten children was born in 1905 near Kosse in the Central Texas county of Limestone. The proud parents named their son James Robert, but everyone called him Jim Rob.

The oldest of the brood was eight years old when the family relocated to the wide-open spaces of the Panhandle. He did the rest of his growing up on ranches in Hall County.

As the son and grandson of fiddlers, Wills took to the instrument like a fish to water. The youngster must have been something of a rural prodigy because at the age of ten he was good enough to stand in for his drunken father at a local dance.

While still in his teens, Wills was already playing his own special kind of music—a unique blend of fiddle-driven frontier folk and the blues and jazz he absorbed from black cotton pickers.

Married at eighteen to his first wife, Edna, Wills learned barbering to keep a roof over their heads. With a baby on the way in 1929, the couple moved to Fort Worth, where the breadwinner hoped to earn more money cutting hair.

Instead, the expectant father found work more to his liking as a fiddle player in a medicine show. When he quit the next year to form his own band, the future star dropped "Jim Rob" in favor of just plain "Bob," the name millions of fans would come to know him by.

Bob Wills in a 1947 publicity shot at the peak of his popularity. *RGD5-B001-F0014-465, Houston Public Library, HMRC.*

Besides its namesake, the Bob Wills Fiddle Band was composed of Herman Arnspiger, the guitarist from the medicine show; singer Milton Brown and Brown's brother Durwood. After their radio debut and first-place finish in a band competition, the foursome changed their name to the Aladdin Laddies in deference to a new sponsor.

The relationship with the lamp manufacturer lasted only a year, but the group was adopted on the rebound by a flour company. As the Light Crust Doughboys, they had a daily show on the radio with a politically ambitious salesman for an emcee.

Milton Brown jumped W. Lee "Pappy" O'Daniels's tight ship in 1932. Considered by some as the cocreator of Western swing, Brown was robbed of a chance to stake an indisputable claim to that fact due to a fatal car crash four years later.

Wills's recurrent battle with the bottle, a problem that plagued him all his life, resulted in his firing by the soon-to-be governor. He took singer Tommy Duncan with him and pieced together the nucleus of the Texas Playboys.

Encouraged by early success in Waco, Wills headed north to Oklahoma, where he put down permanent roots in 1934. The Playboys became a lunchtime fixture on 50,000-watt KVOO, a Tulsa station that broadcast their toe-tapping tunes across the Southwest.

Wills proved to be not only a musical innovator but also an uncanny judge of talent. To go along with silky smooth baritone Duncan, he added Leon McAuliffe on steel guitar, drummer Smokey Dacus, piano player Al Stricklin and guitarist Jesse Ashlock.

To a tireless tinkerer like Wills, the Playboys were always a work in progress. As famoustexans.com explains, "The earliest incarnations of the group...included trumpets and saxophones, and at various times, female vocalists with an Andrews Sisters style. The band's makeup and size changed frequently. It could grow into a veritable western symphony or shrink to a tight little fiddle band."

The icing on the entertaining cake was the bandleader himself. Wills's nonstop patter was meant to do more than amuse the audience. It was his unselfish way of sharing the spotlight with solo performers, which came to include practically every Playboy.

Despite a six-days-a-week radio commitment, Thursday and Saturday live shows at a Tulsa ballroom, frequent tours and recording sessions, Wills found time to marry and divorce four different women between 1936 and 1941. Then in 1942, he walked down the aisle with Betty Anderson, who remained his wife until the day he died.

The 1940 release of "New San Antonio Rose" sold a million copies and established a nationwide fan base for Wills and the Playboys. While most members were in the service during World War II, their leader, discharged for medical reasons, appeared in the first of nineteen motion pictures.

The postwar period was Wills's most productive and profitable. The popular Playboys drew bigger crowds than the Tommy Dorsey and Benny Goodman bands, enabling him to gross $500,000 a year.

What money Wills did not spend, the soft touch gave to friends and total strangers. By the early 1950s, he was drowning in red ink and owed the IRS a fortune in back taxes.

From then on, Bob Wills's life was no bed of roses. The struggle to pay off creditors and the government took a terrible toll on his health. Heart attacks in 1962 and 1964 were followed by a stroke in 1969 that left him partially disabled and struggling to speak.

In December 1973, Wills felt well enough to attend a special two-day reunion of the Playboys during which a final album titled *For the Last Time* would be recorded. He took part in the initial session but overnight suffered another stroke that left him in a coma.

The "King of Western Swing" never regained consciousness and passed away a year and a half later in May 1975.

43

# CHILL WILLS

## *Westerns His Bread and Butter*

Theodore Childress Wills was born in 1903 at Seagoville on the eastern outskirts of Dallas. While he liked to claim that his parents called him "Chill" because he arrived on the hottest day of the year, it was merely an abbreviated form of his middle name.

An entertainer while still in short pants, he started in vaudeville and on the dramatic stage before breaking into the movies in the 1930s with his own singing group, Chill Wills and the Avalon Boys.

Wills was soon flying solo and in a few short years became one of filmdom's most familiar faces without ever landing a leading role. The character actor brought to the screen an amiable personality, which was "sometimes shrewd, sometimes funny, but always talkative and philosophizing" to quote one Hollywood historian.

A busy performer who was rarely out of work, Wills made mostly Westerns of the A variety. In 1941 alone, he appeared in *The Westerner* with Gary Cooper and Walter Brennan, *Western Union* with Randolph Scott and Robert Young, *The Bad Man* with Wallace Beery and Lionel Barrymore and *Belle Starr* with Randolph Scott and Gene Tierney.

But Wills took pains to avoid being typecast as a sagebrush second fiddle. In the World War II decade, his non-Western credits included major motion pictures like *Boom Town*, *Meet Me in St. Louis* and *The Harvey Girls*.

In the 1950s, Wills was the voice of Francis the Talking Mule in six comedies, but Westerns remained his stock in trade. Some of the titles, though by no means all, were *The Sundowners*, *Rock Island Trail*, *High Lonesome*,

*Cattle Drive*, *Bronco Buster*, *Ride the Man Down*, *Tumbleweed*, *Timberjack*, *Kentucky Rifle*, *Gun for a Coward* and *From Hell to Texas*.

Wills turned in his finest performance to date in *Giant*, the 1957 epic based on the Edna Ferber novel and starring Rock Hudson, Elizabeth Taylor and James Dean. His unusually understated portrayal of a Texas rancher received favorable reviews, but it was another member of the supporting cast, Mercedes McCambridge, that was nominated for an Oscar.

Wills got a call in early 1960 from old friend John Wayne. Duke was finally realizing his lifelong dream of making a movie about the Alamo and wanted Wills for the part of Beekeeper, Davy Crockett's comic-relief sidekick.

Wayne had better luck with Wills, who jumped at the chance, than with the casting of two top roles. He had his heart set on Clark Gable as William Travis and Burt Lancaster as Jim Bowie, but neither could work the project into their schedules. That was how British actor Laurence Harvey and Richard Widmark wound up playing the immortal heroes.

Once the expensive film, which cost $4.5 million more than the original budget, was in the can, Wayne launched the most aggressive Oscar campaign Hollywood had ever seen. In his mind, it was not enough for *The Alamo* to cash in at the box office. His pride and joy had to sweep the Academy Awards.

Wayne's high-powered publicist pulled out all the stops. He hung a huge banner over Hollywood Boulevard with a quote from Duke's mentor, director John Ford: "This is the most important motion picture ever made. It is timeless. It will run forever."

*The Alamo* was nominated for Best Picture and four technical awards. The one acting nomination went not to Wayne, Harvey, Widmark or Richard Boone, who played Sam Houston, but to Chill Wills for Best Supporting Actor.

Wills followed Wayne's example by hiring his own promoter, but the best he could afford was a former prison physical education teacher named "Bow-Wow" Wojciechowicz. Among the advertisements the shameless huckster put in *Variety* and other trade publications was a full page of testimonials from the rich and famous back in Texas and another with a snapshot of Wills saying, "Win, lose or draw, you're still my cousins and I love you all."

Groucho Marx had a little fun at the Texan's expense. "Dear Mr. Wills, I am delighted to be your cousin but I am voting for Sal Mineo."

Wojciechowicz responded with a buckskinned Wills superimposed on a group photograph of *The Alamo* cast. The controversial caption read:

On screen and off, Chill Wills called everybody "cousin." *RGD5F6506, Houston Public Library, HMRC.*

"We are praying—harder than the real Texans prayed for their lives at the Alamo—for Chill Wills to win the Oscar."

The tasteless commercial shocked and angered practically everybody from Hollywood to Houston. Texas newspapers were swamped by outraged letters to the editor, and even John Wayne chastised Wills in print.

After Peter Ustinov took home the Best Supporting Actor award for *Spartacus*, Wills told a columnist exactly what he thought of Wojciechowicz: "I always had a very reputable name in this town. I'll get even with that so-and-so if it's the last thing I do."

When the dust had settled, Wills was relieved to learn he still had a career in the movies. The parts were fewer and farther between, but that had more to do with his age and the declining popularity of the traditional Western than a "Bow-Wow" Wojciechowicz backlash.

In fact, Chill Wills kept working on the big and small screens right up until 1978, the year cancer took his life.

# SOURCES

As was the case with my most recent book, *Unforgettable Texans*, the chapters in *Texas Entertainers: Lone Stars in Profile* first saw the light of day as newspaper columns over the past thirty-five years. Understandably, that makes a comprehensive list of sources all but impossible to compile, and besides, it would be downright dull reading.

However, for readers interested into delving more deeply into the history of the Lone Star State and the lives of the men and women who forged the Texas we live in today, I can recommend several important places to start.

First, be sure to order a copy of the *Texas Almanac* that is now published every other year. The current edition is for 2018–2019, but earlier editions dating back as far as you can afford are available.

Second, the answer to every question you could conceivably ask about Texas can be found in the *Handbook of Texas*. And, lucky you, the online version of this precious resource is as close as your computer and free to use.

Third, the *Southwest Historical Quarterly* going as far back as the turn of the twentieth century is available on the same website as the *Handbook of Texas*. A word of caution: While the more recent issues (from, say, 1970) are layman friendly, the farther back in time you go, you will find the articles were written in a stilted style for an academic or scholarly audience. Therefore, the reading can be tedious and, depending on the subject, decidedly dull. But by choosing those articles that interest you at first glance, you will be richly rewarded.

Fourth and finally, the one must-read for a good basic introduction to Texas history is T.R. Fehrenbach's *Lone Star*. Do not let anyone tell you different. This book is the best place to begin.

# ABOUT THE AUTHOR

Bartee Haile began writing This Week in Texas History in 1983 for small-town and suburban newspapers across the Lone Star State. Thirty-five years and more than 1,800 columns later, it is the most widely read and longest-running feature of its kind.

*Texas Entertainers: Lone Stars in Profile* is his fifth book for The History Press. The master storyteller's earlier titles are *Texas Depression-Era Desperadoes, Murder Most Texan, Texas Boomtowns: A History of Blood and Oil* and *Unforgettable Texans*—all fascinating page-turners.

A fourth- or fifth-generation Texan (like most Texans he cannot say for sure), Bartee Haile lives in the Houston area with his wife, Gerri.